Jamaica
Coloring Book

Adult Colouring Books

Aryla Publishing 2017

Copyright @ 2018 Aryla Publishing All Rights Reserved

No part of this book may be reproduced or transmitted in any form or by means, electronic or mechanical, including photocopying recording or by any information storage and retrieval system without written permission from the publisher

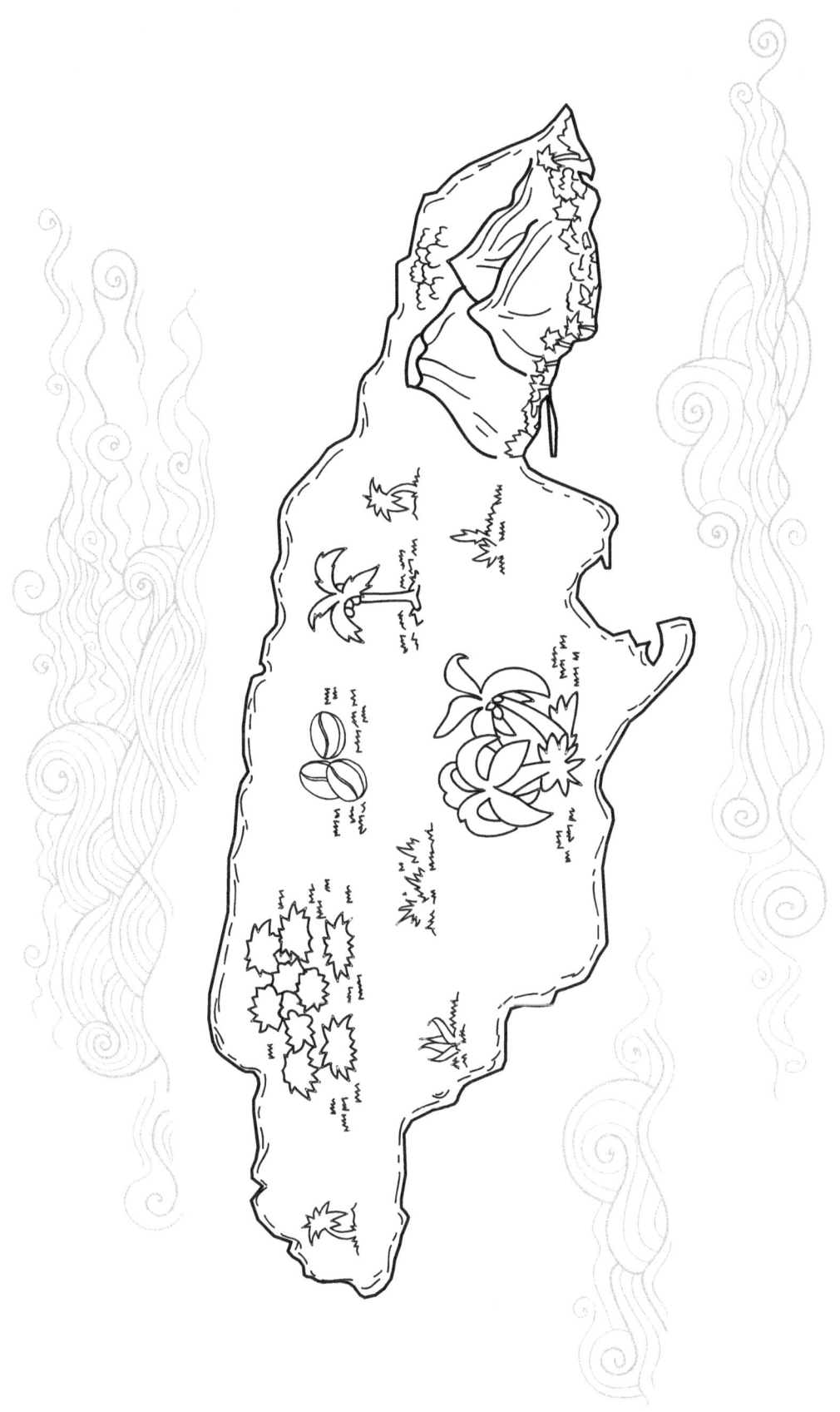

Land we love

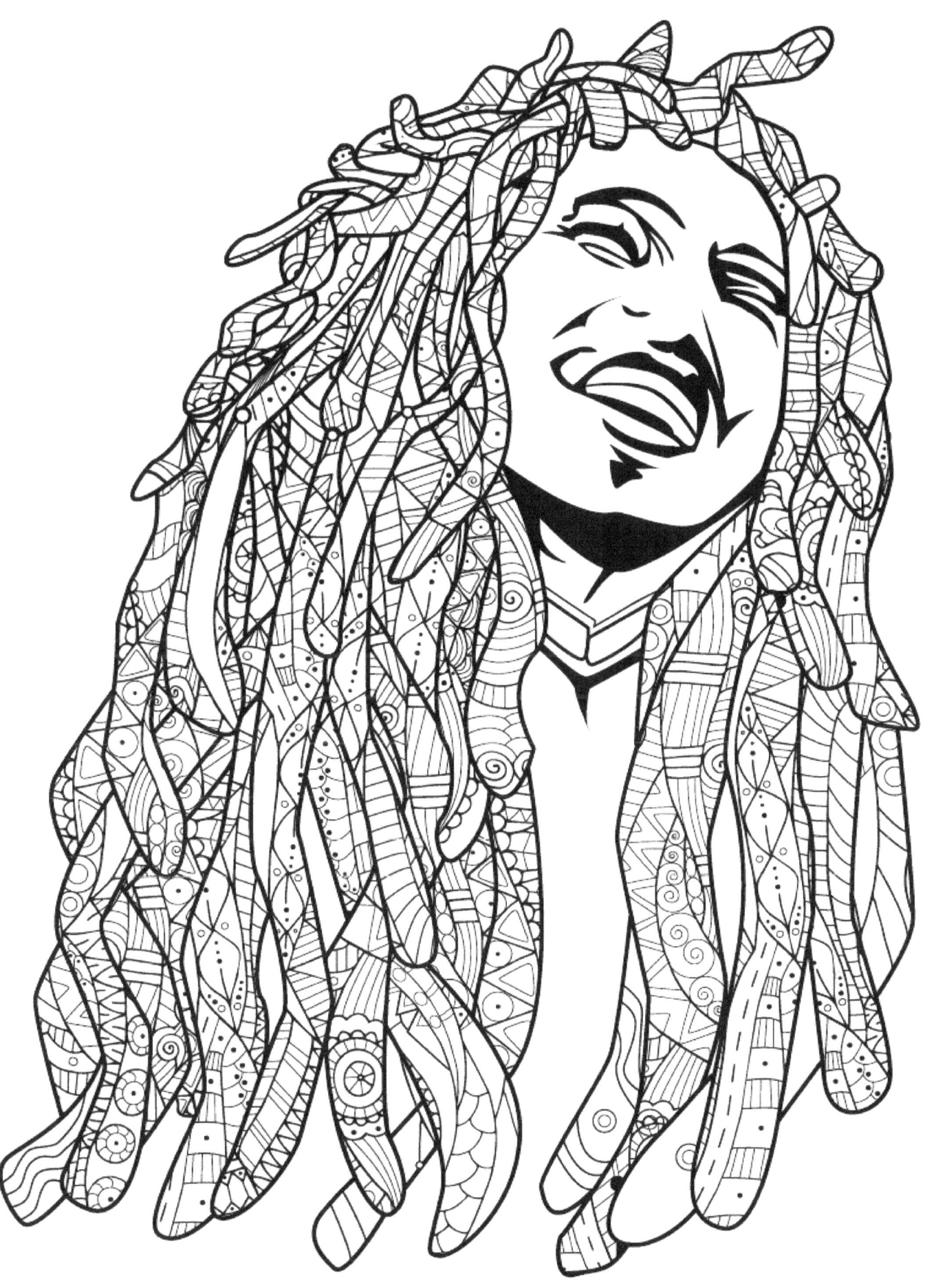

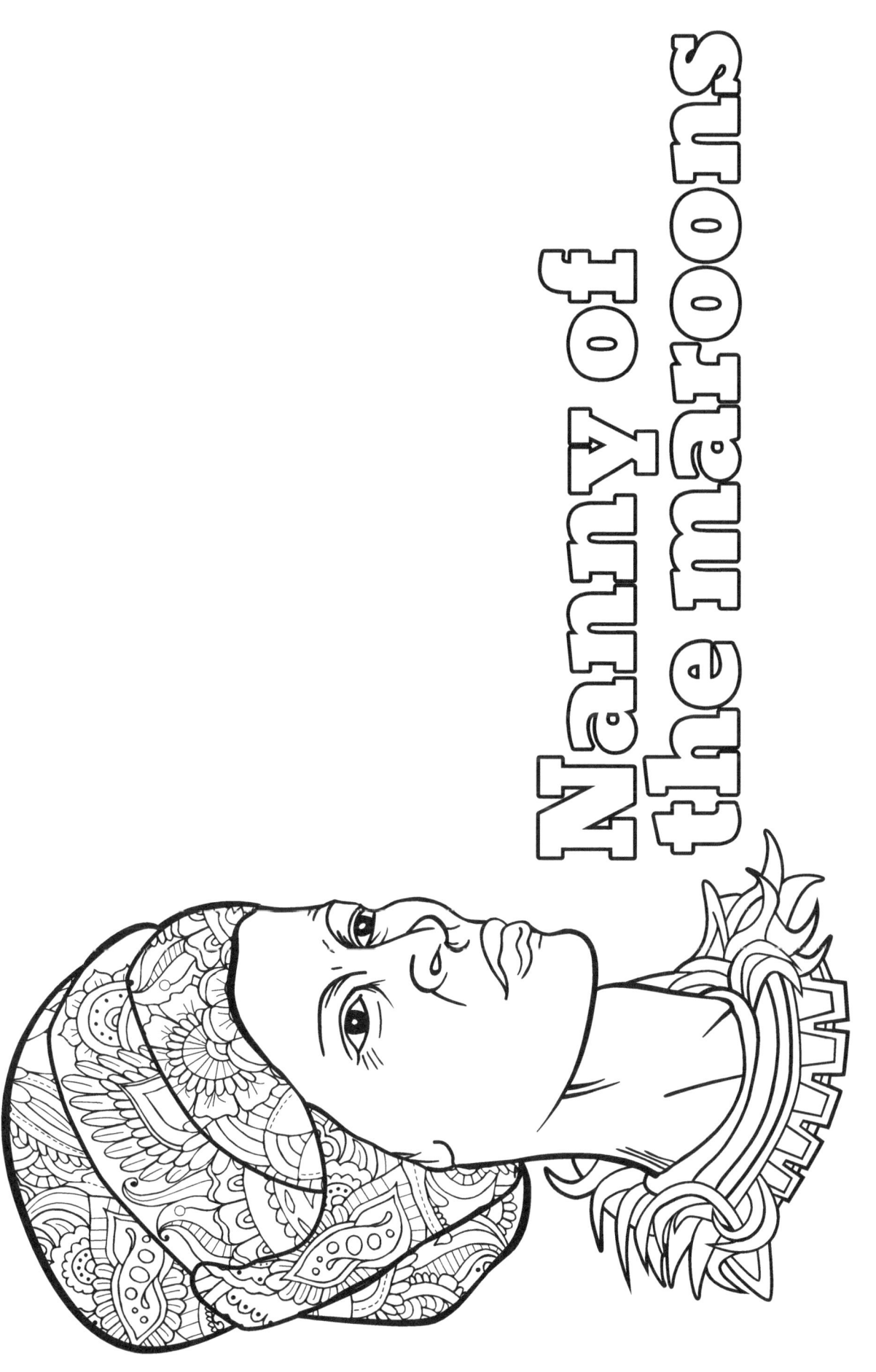

Nanny of the maroons

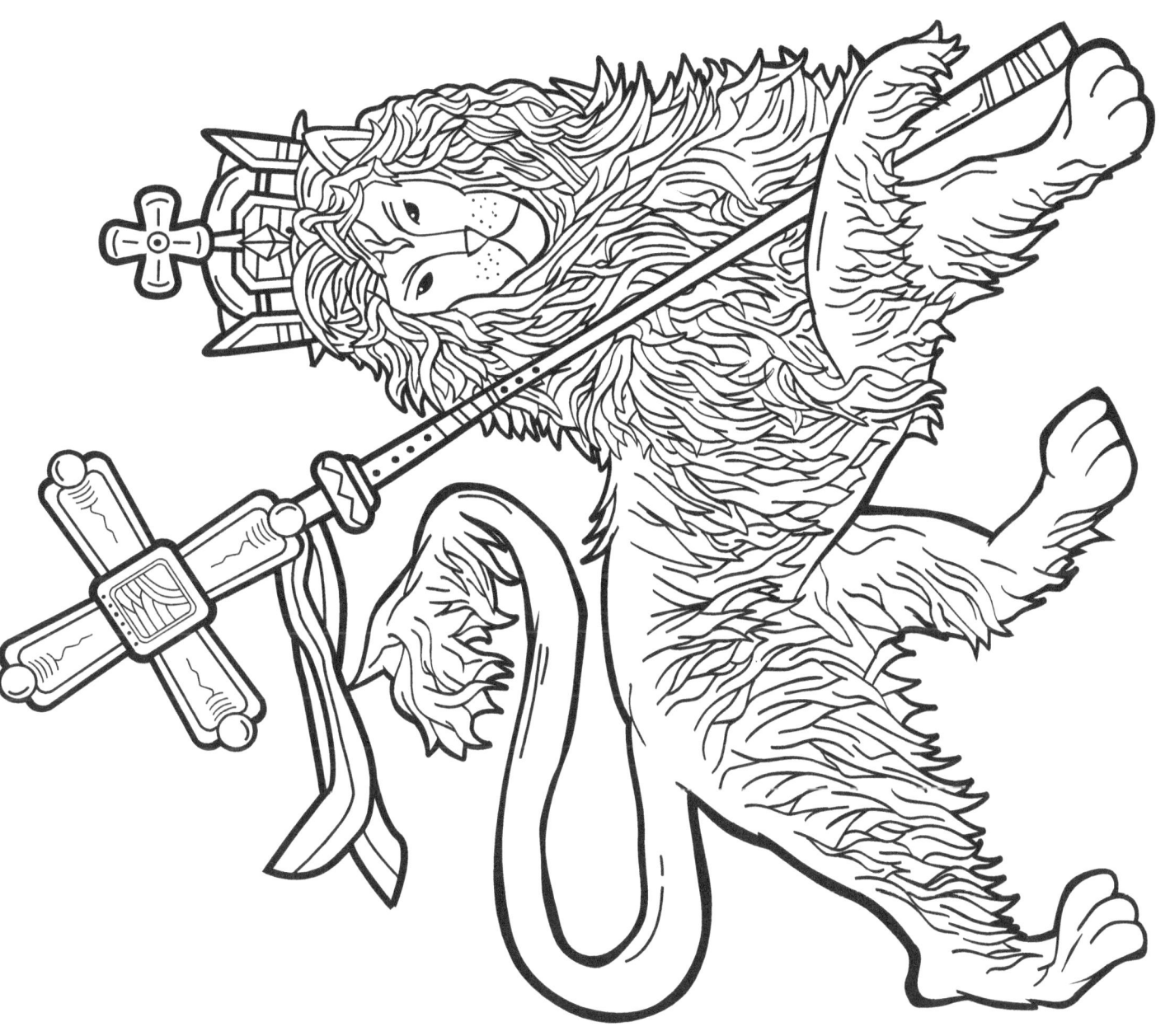

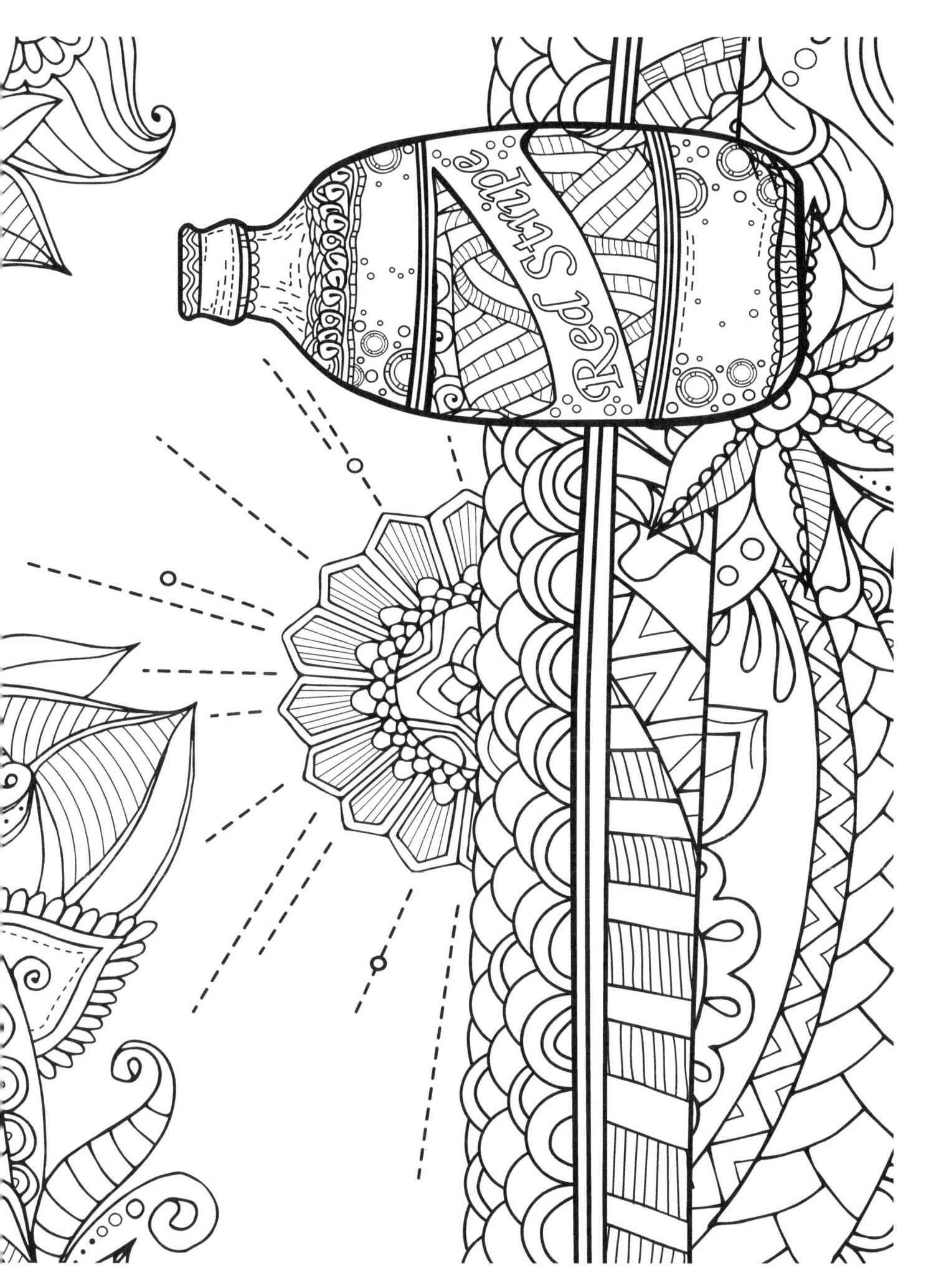

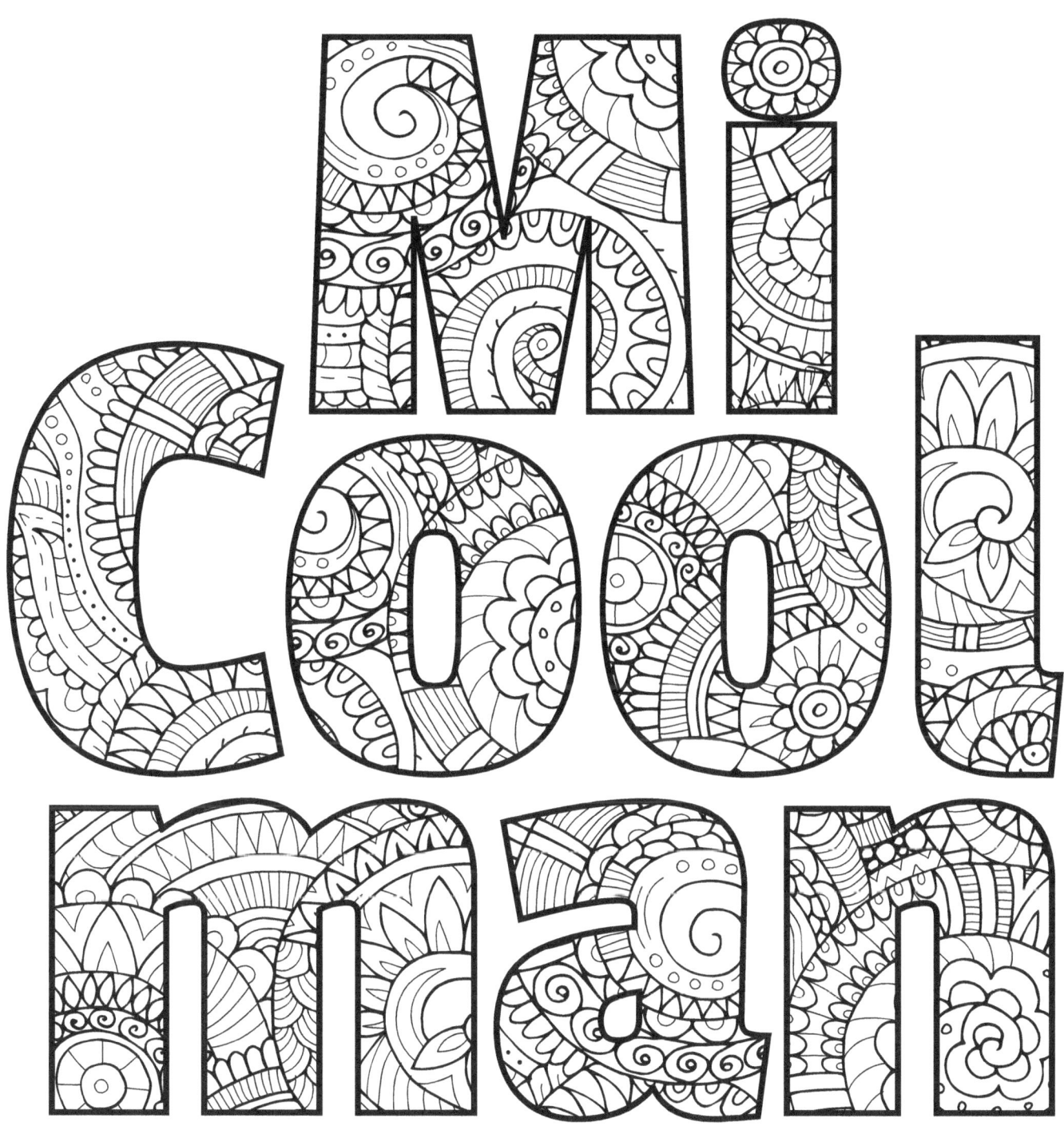

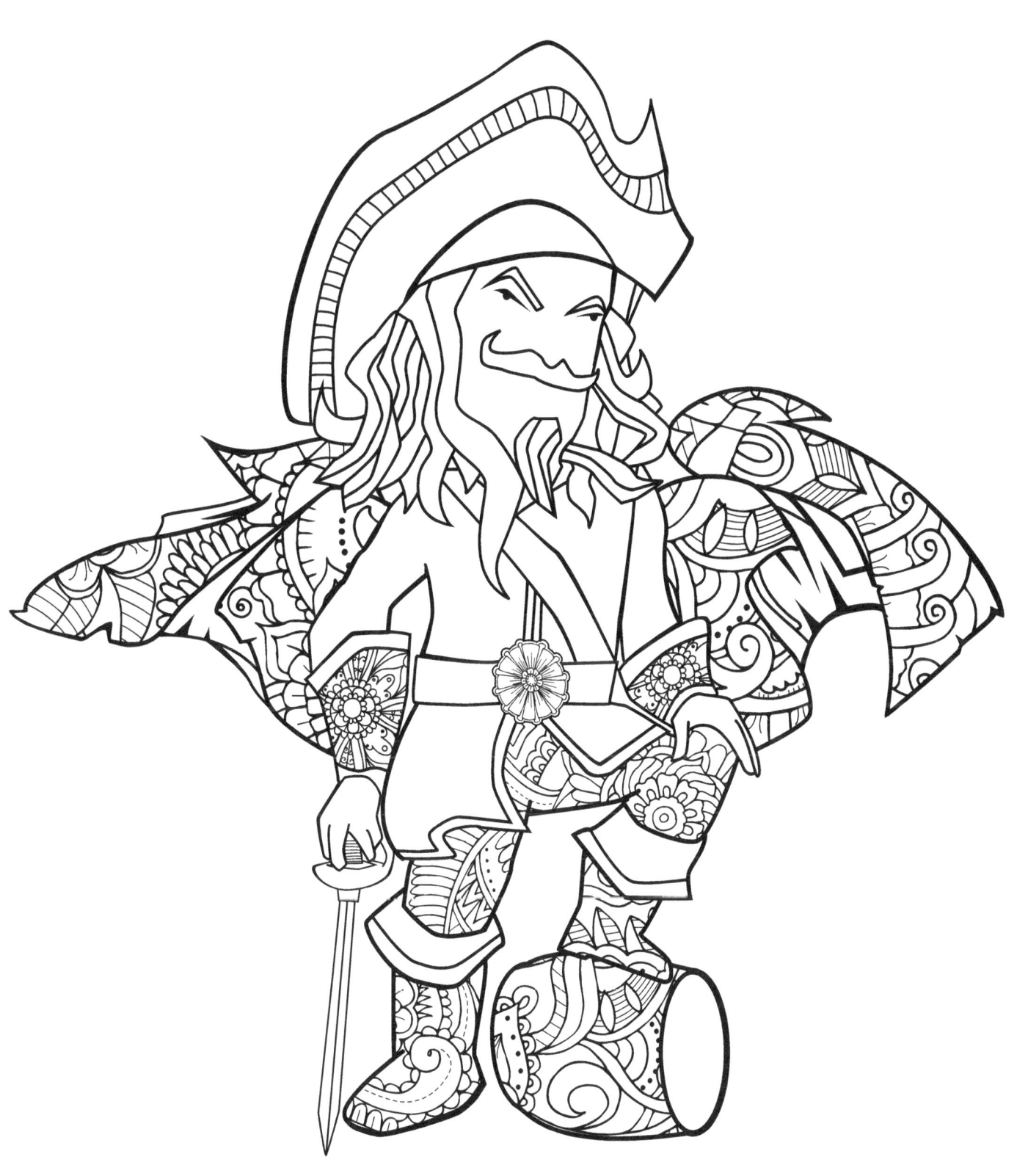

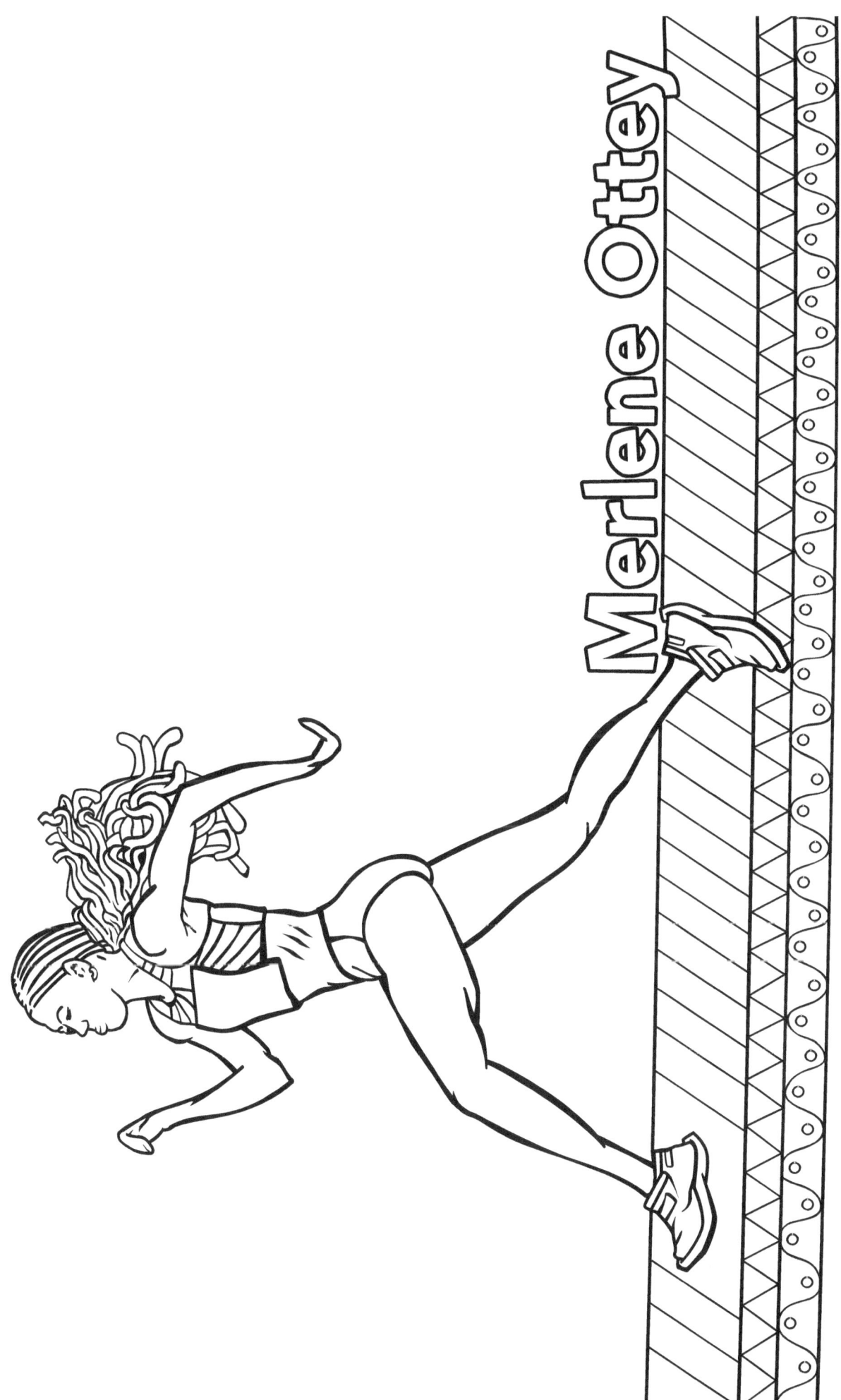

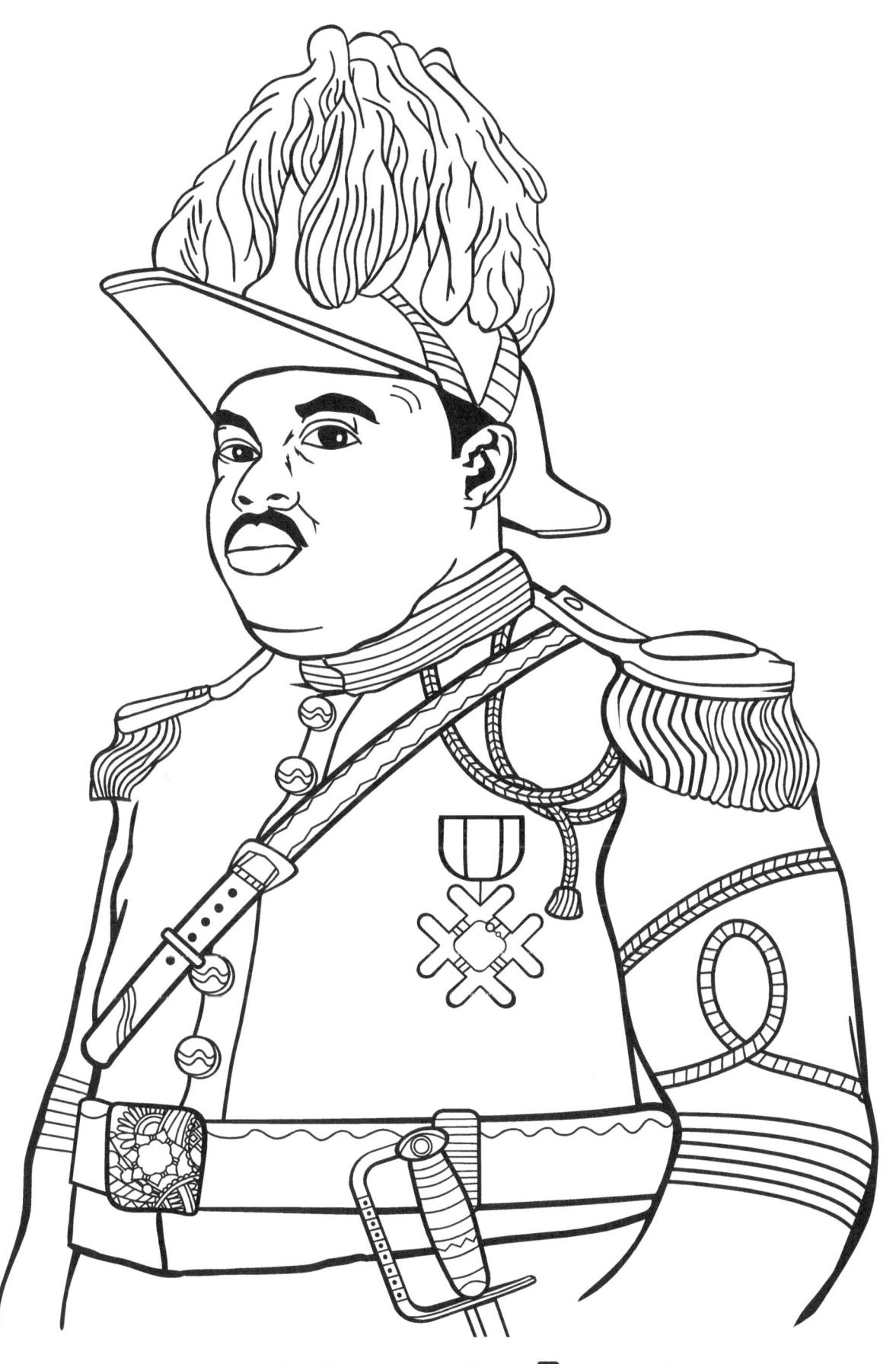

Marcus Mosiah Garvey

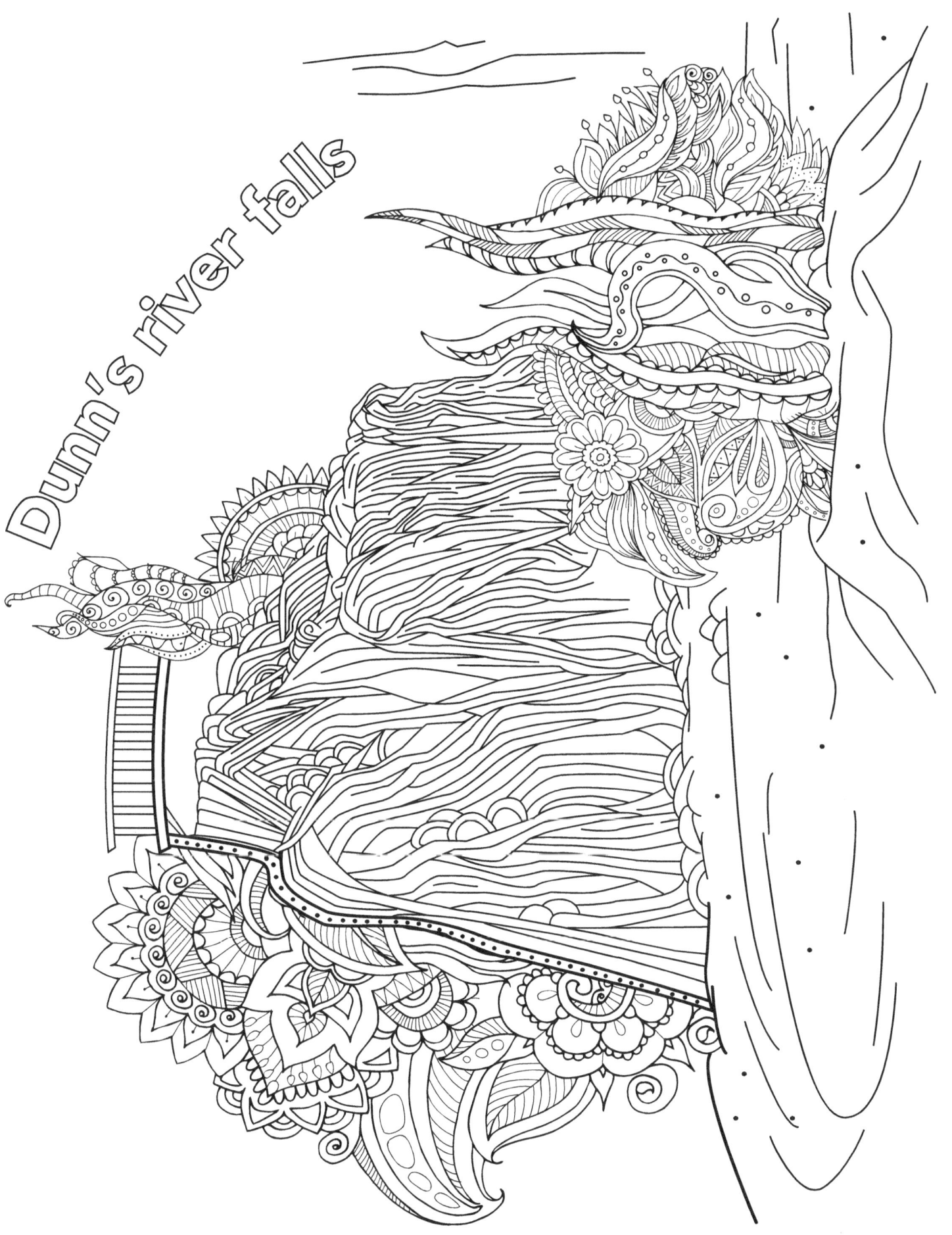
Dunn's river falls

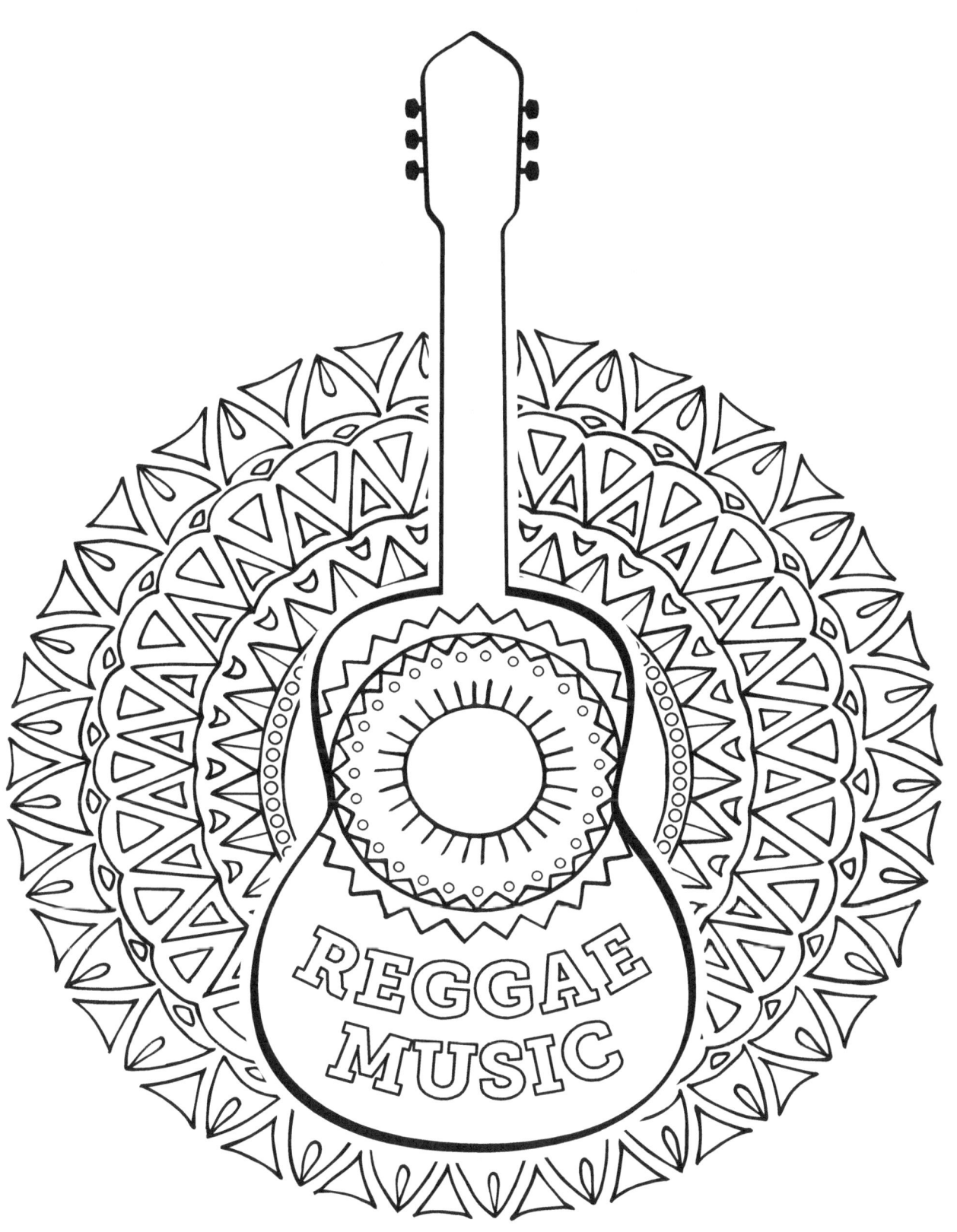

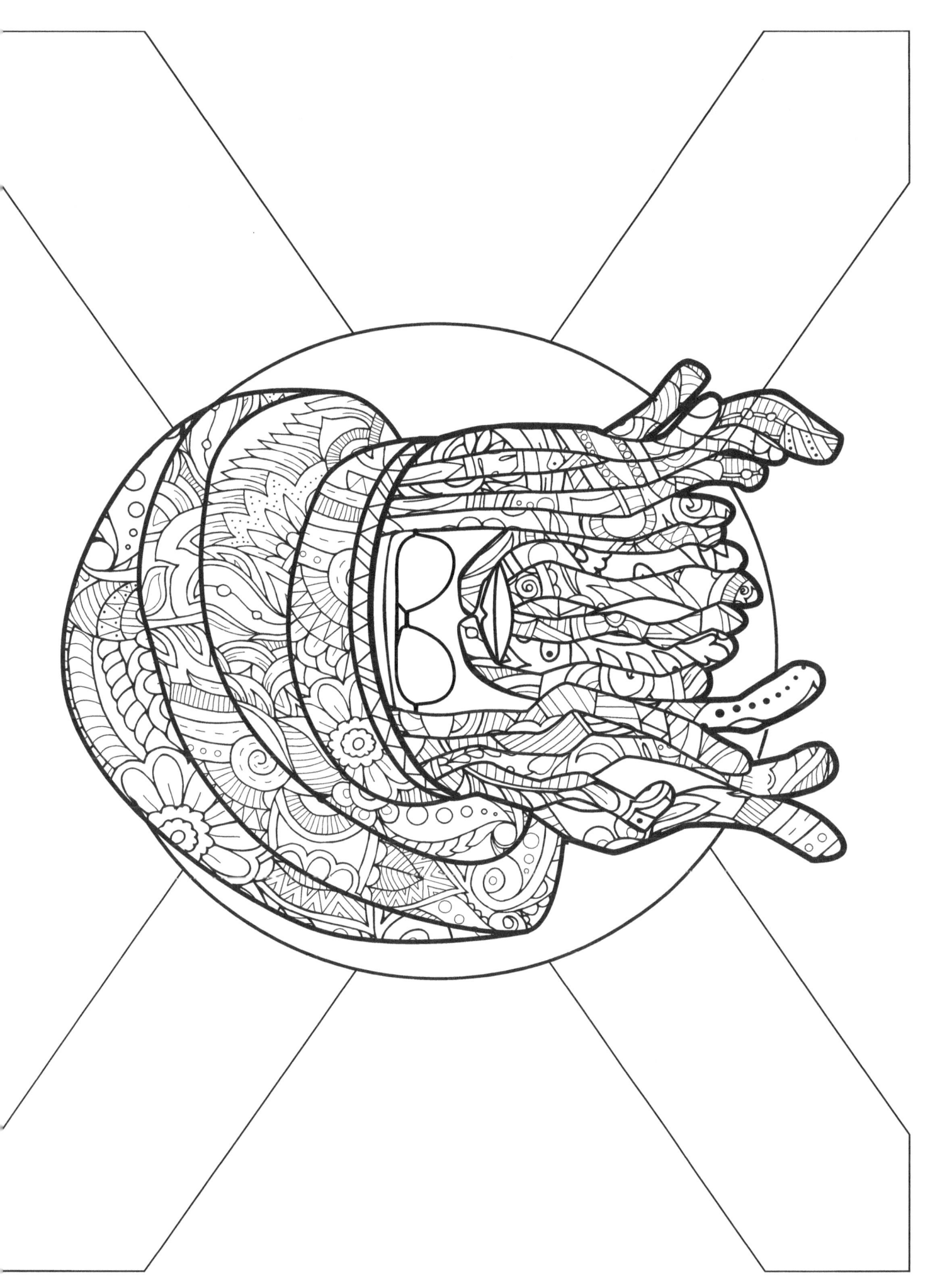

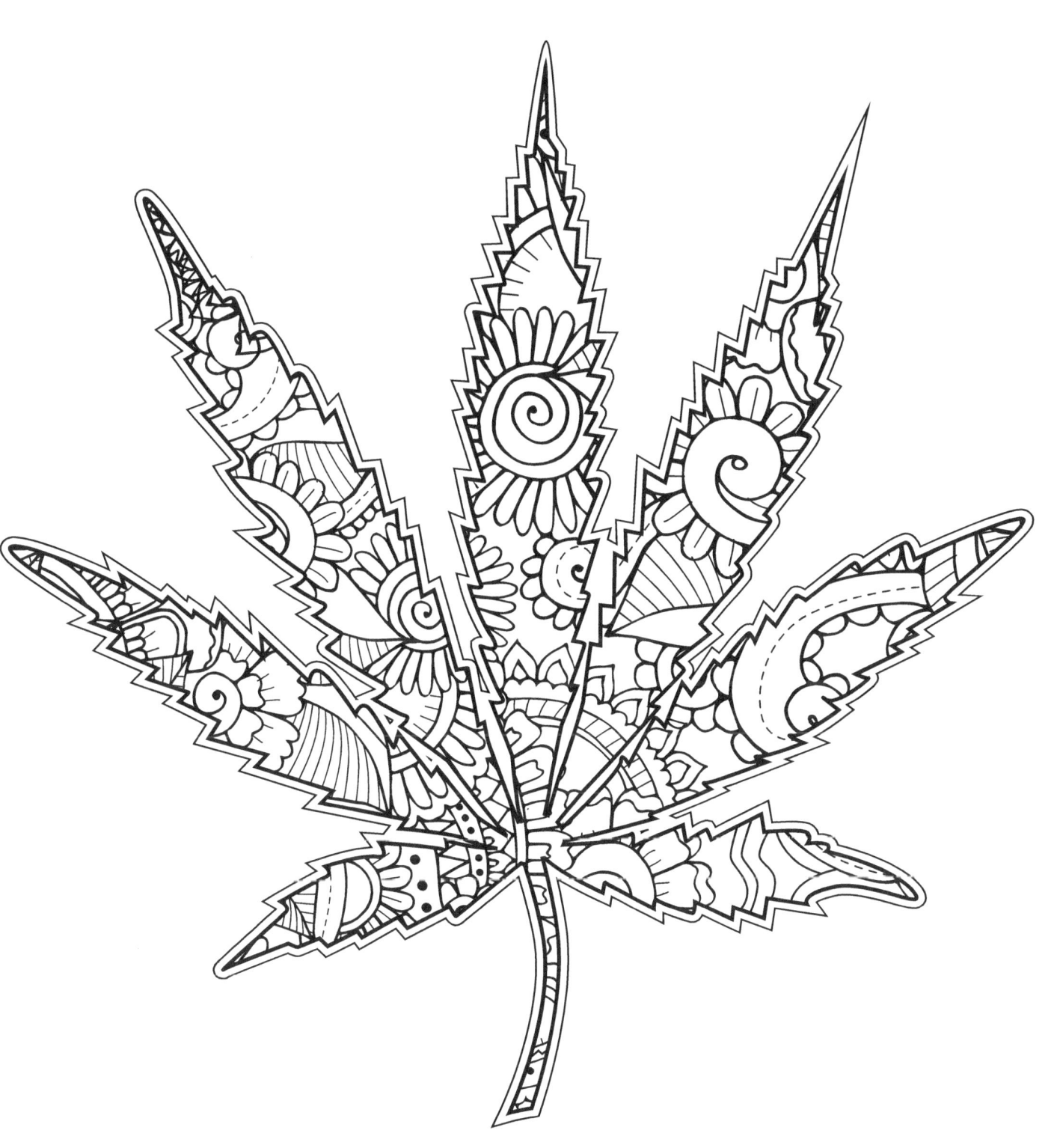

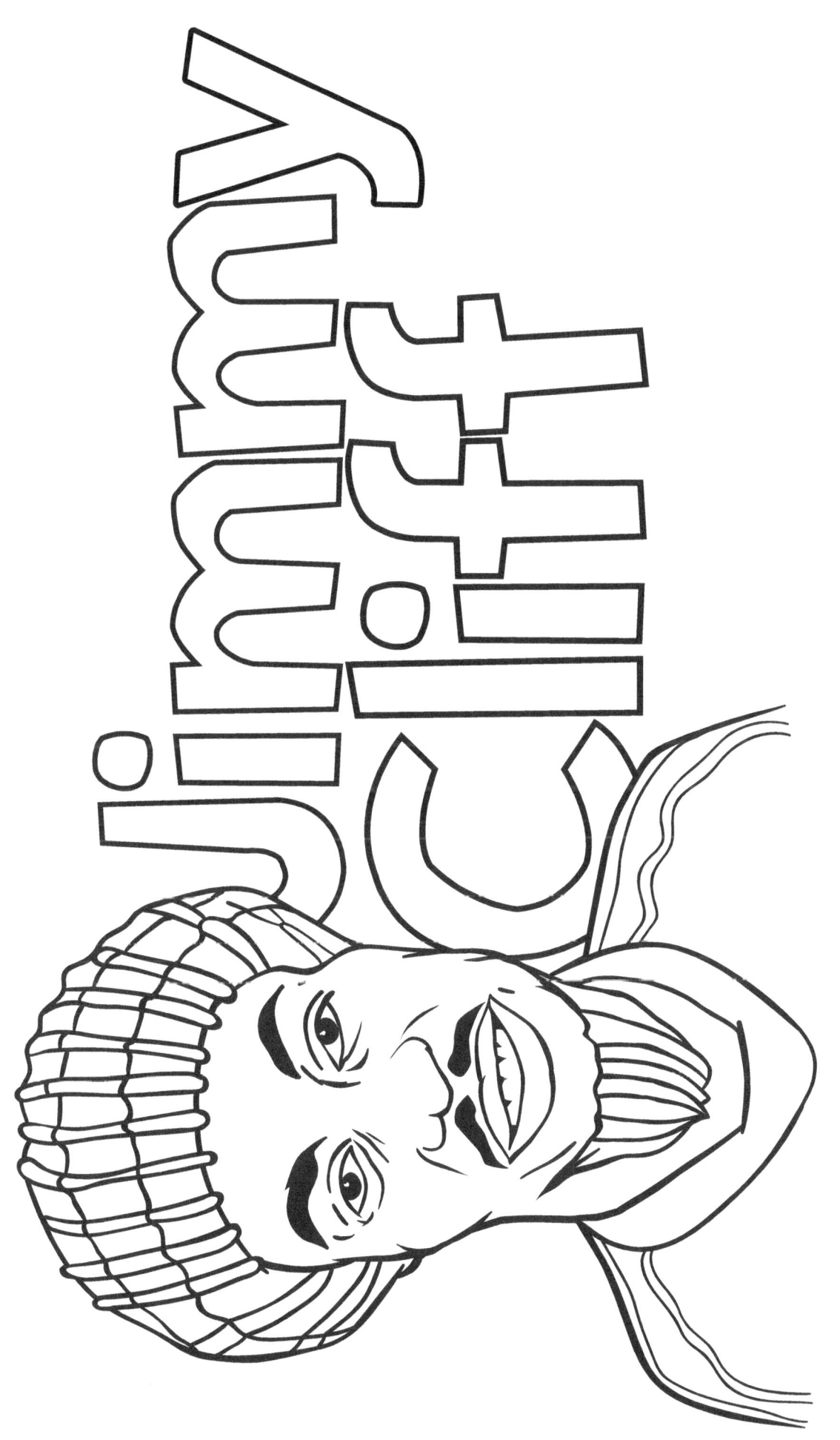

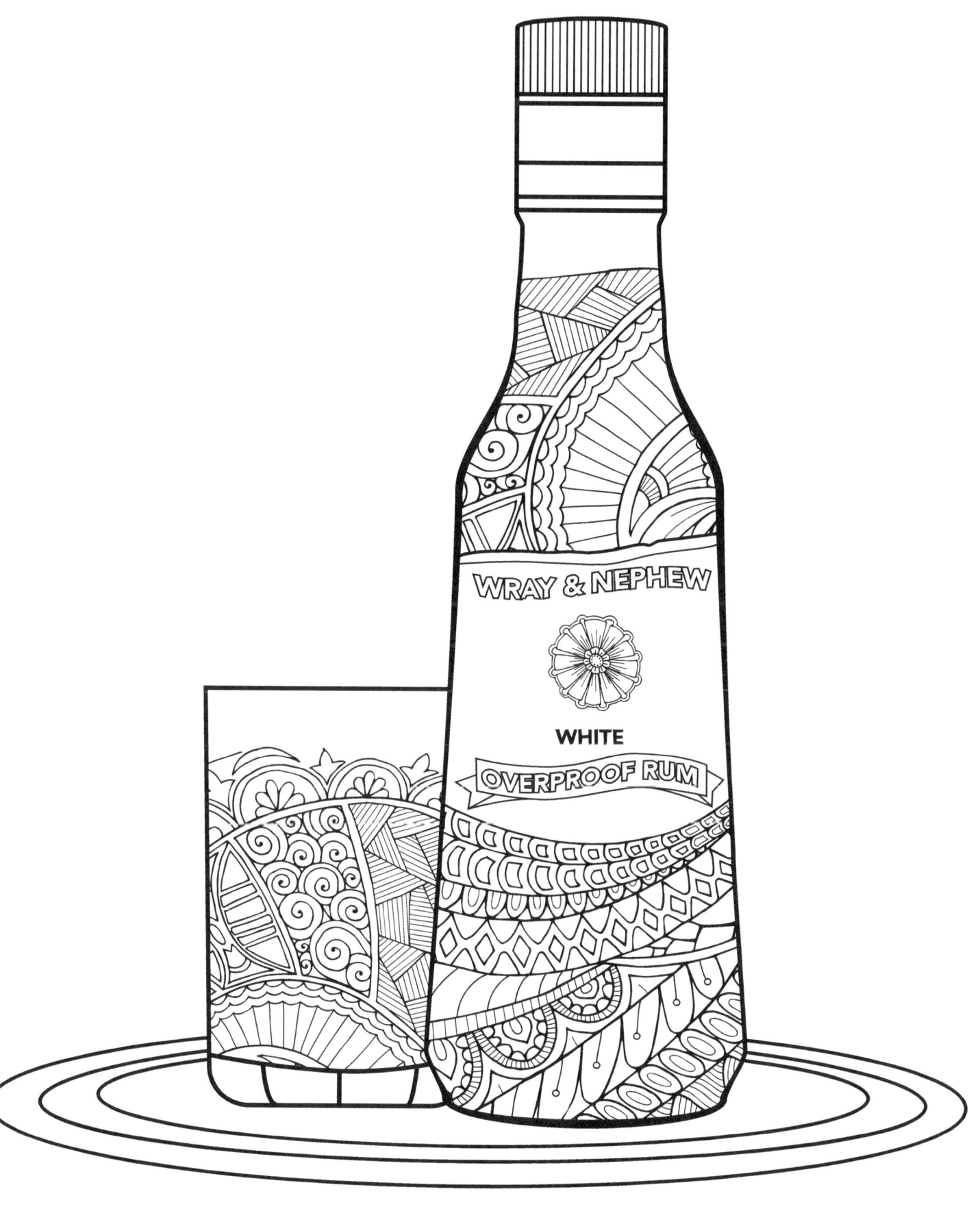

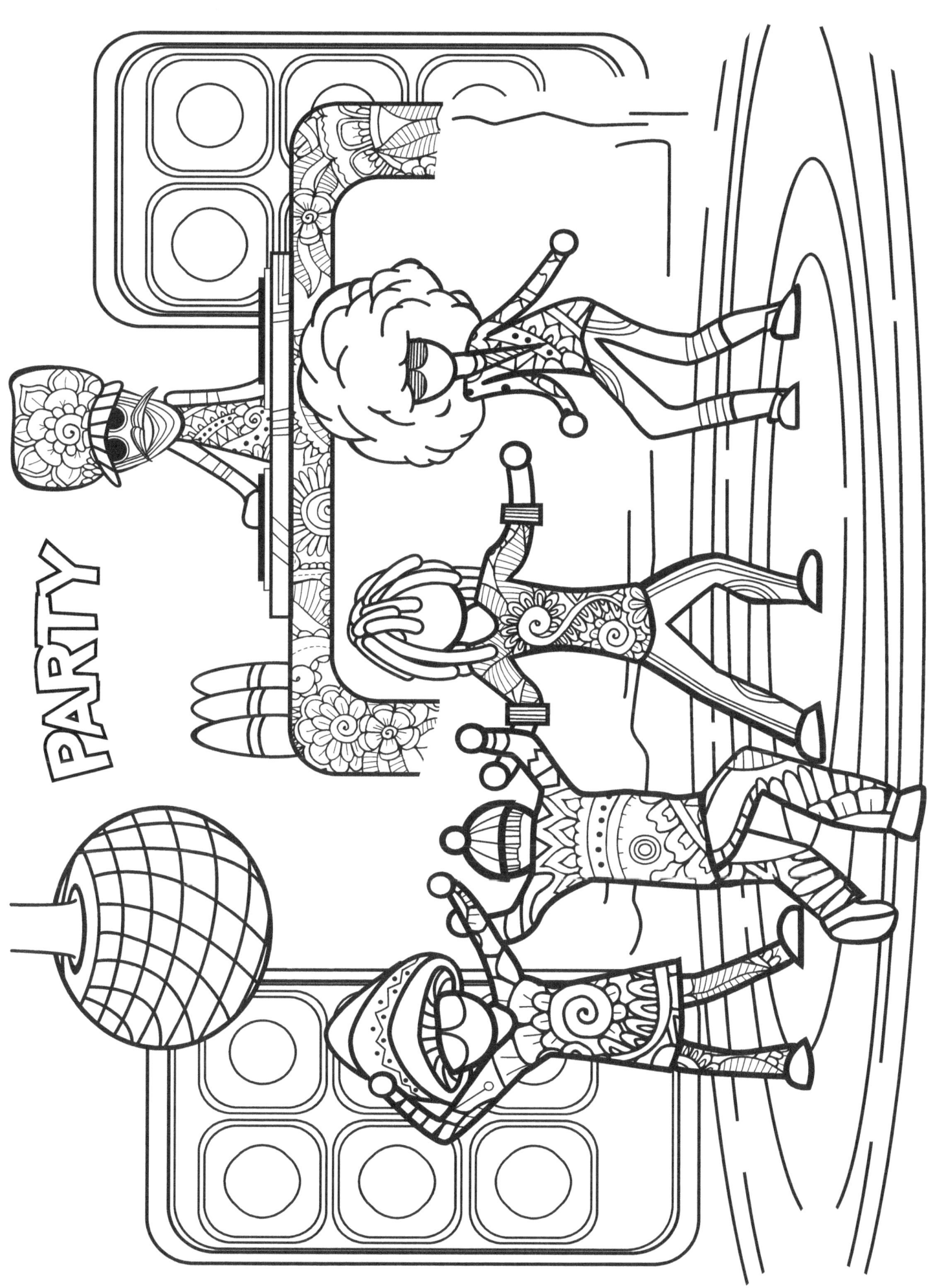

Christopher Columbus

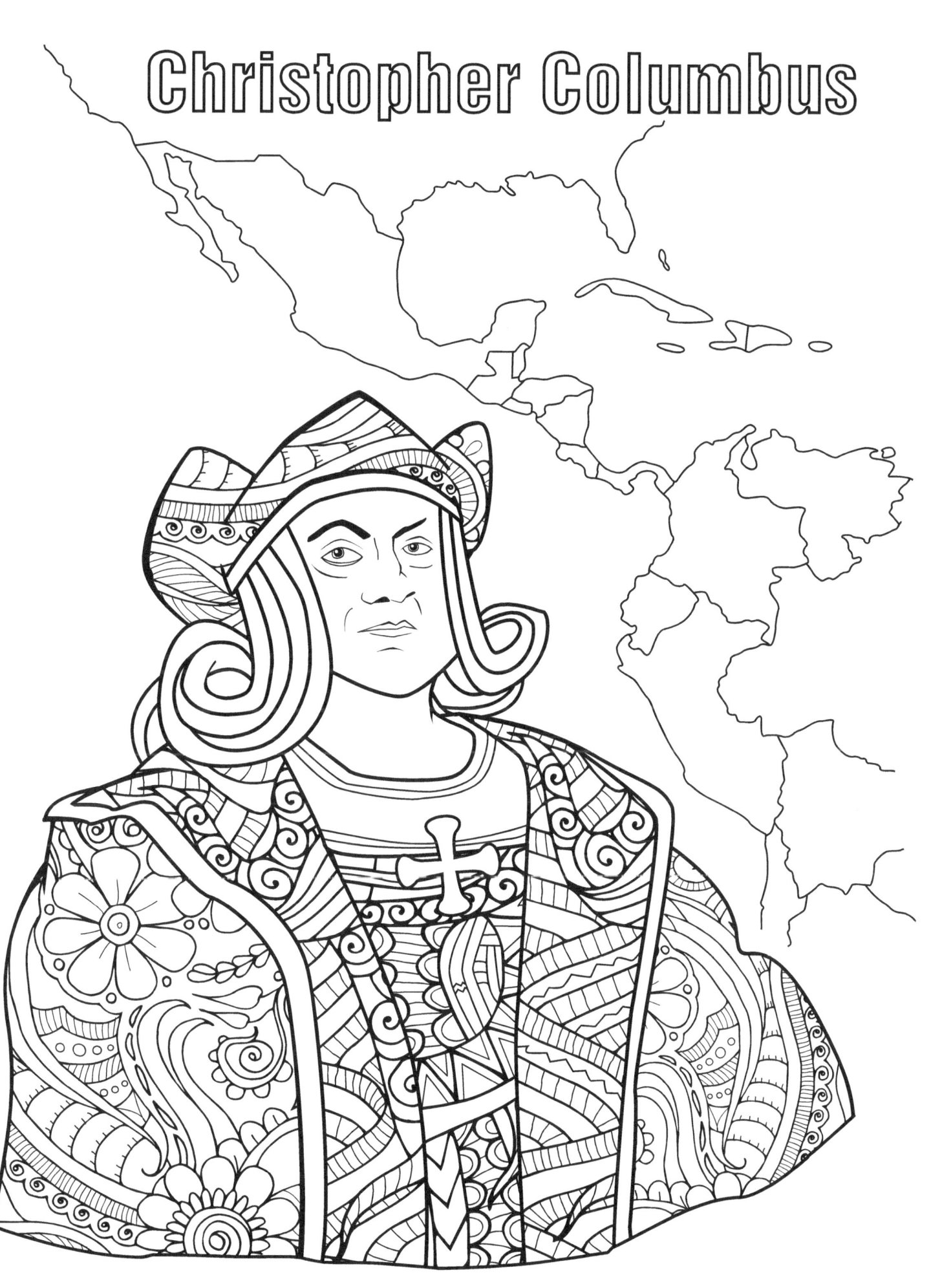

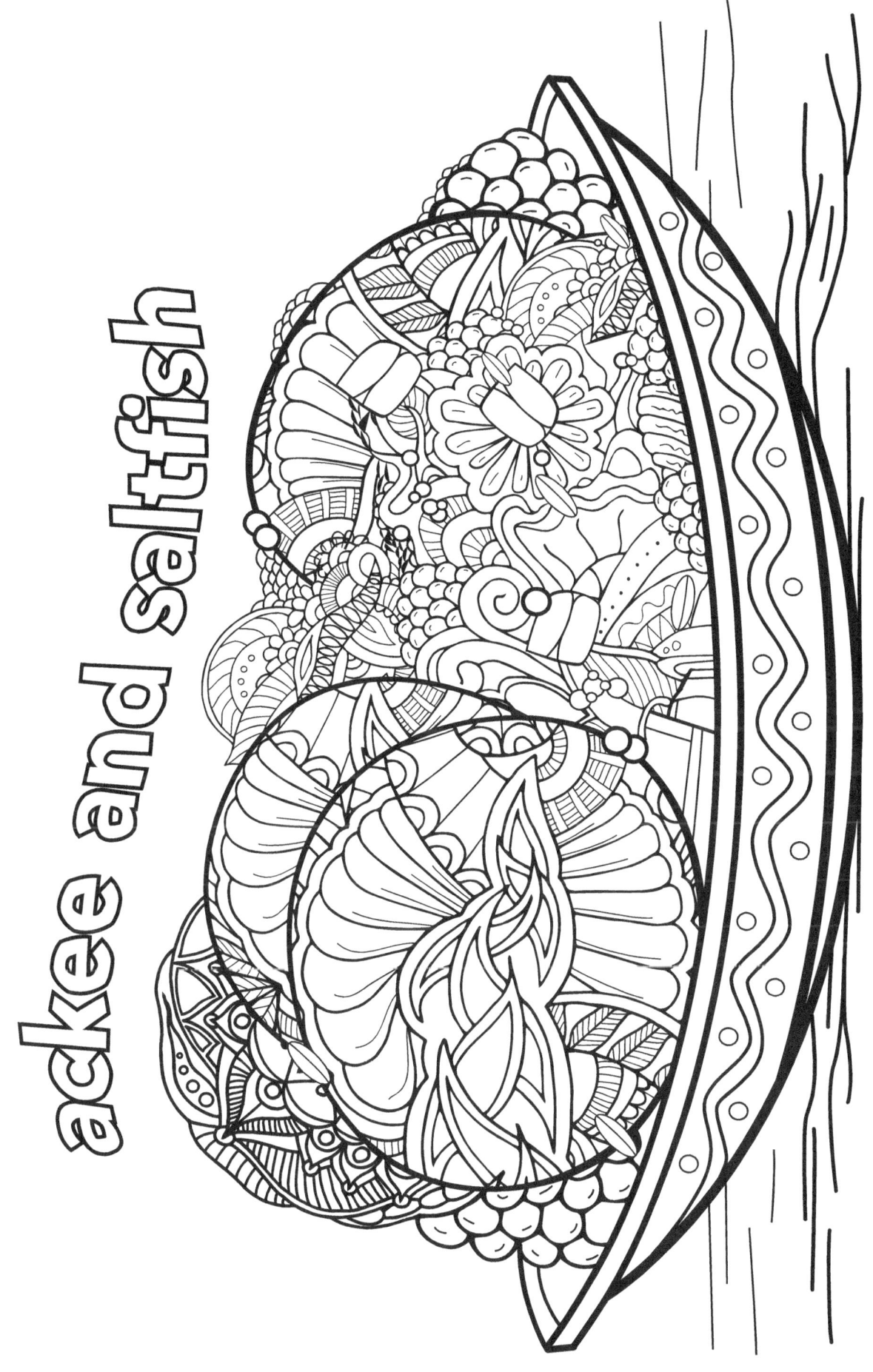

ackee and saltfish

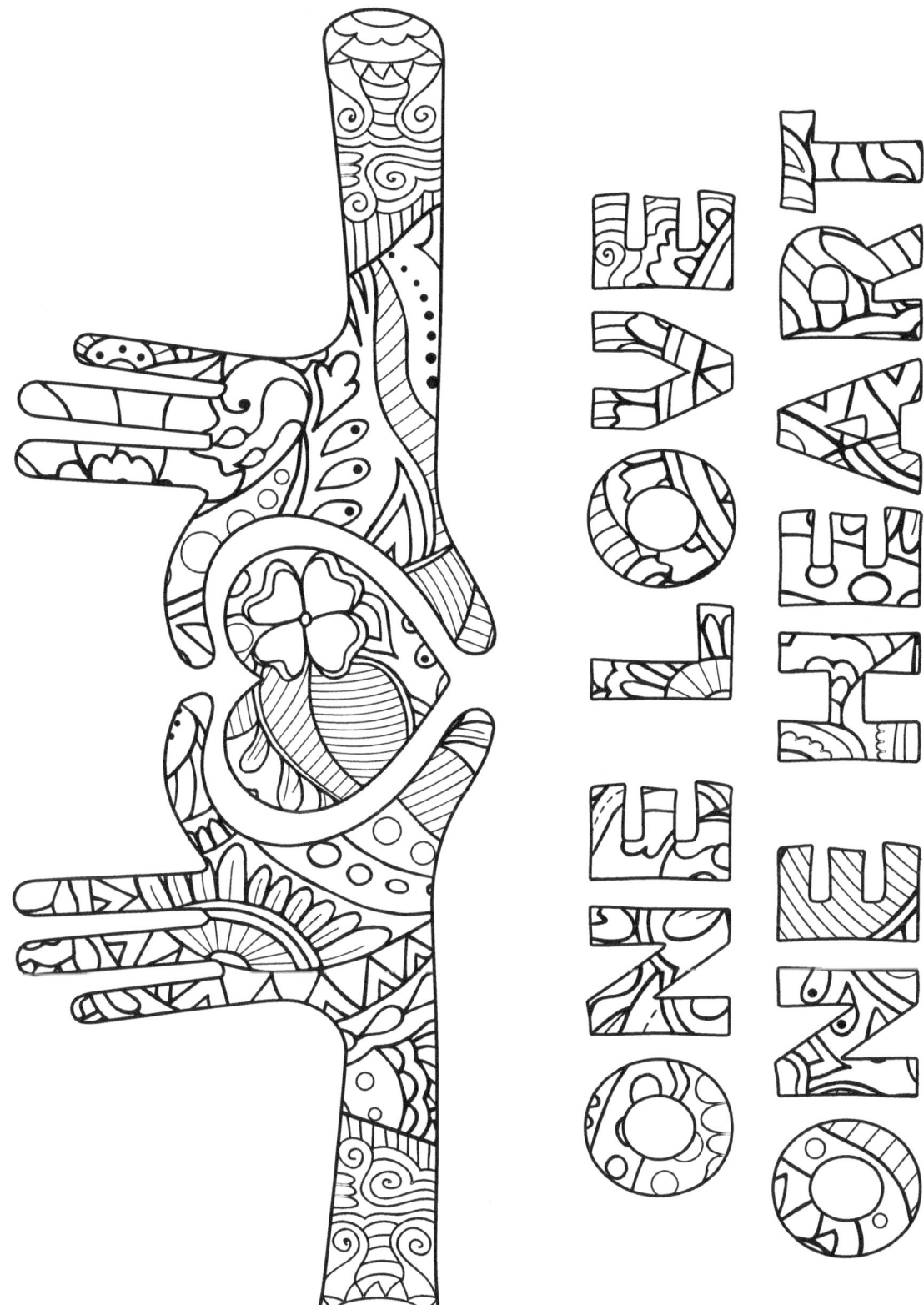

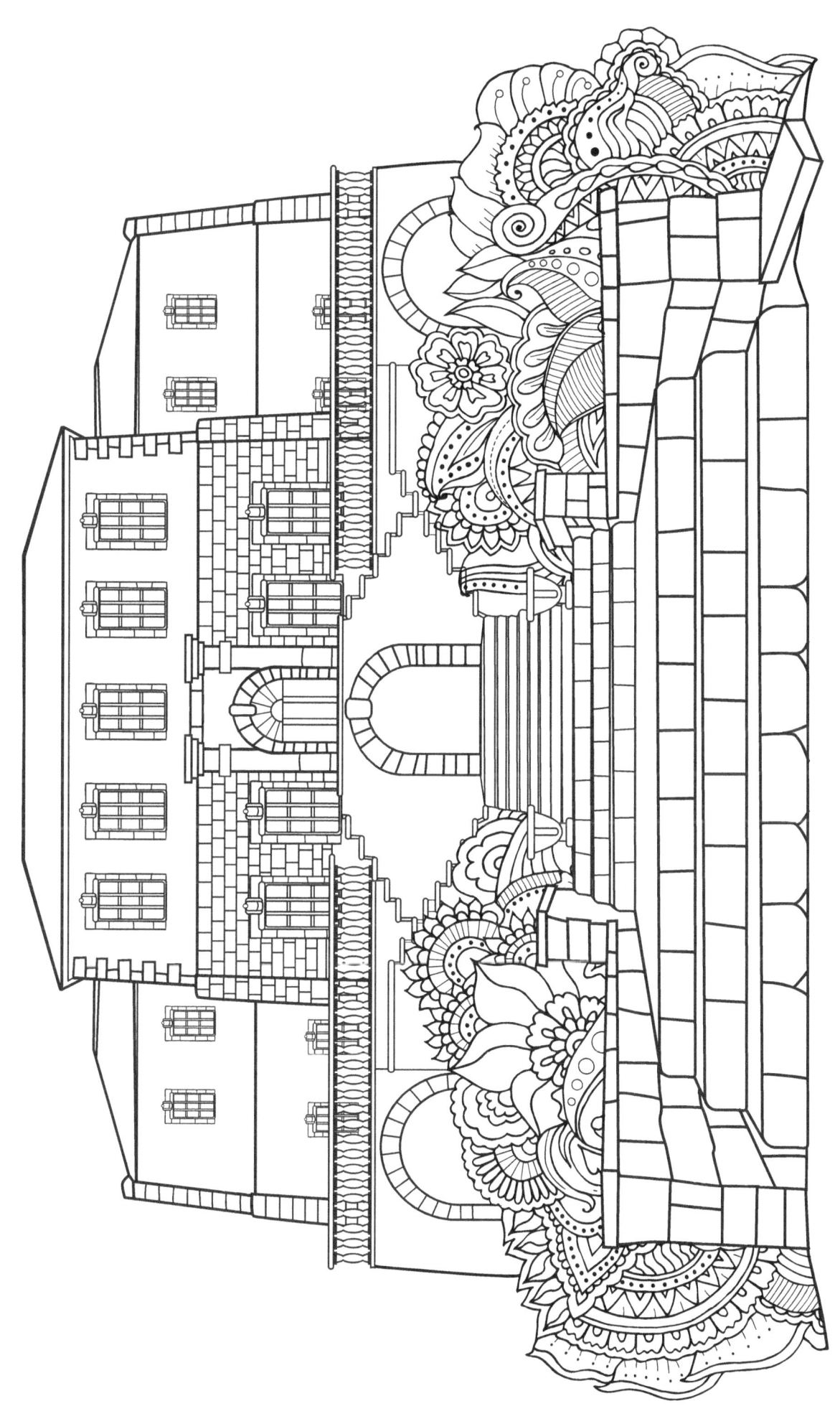

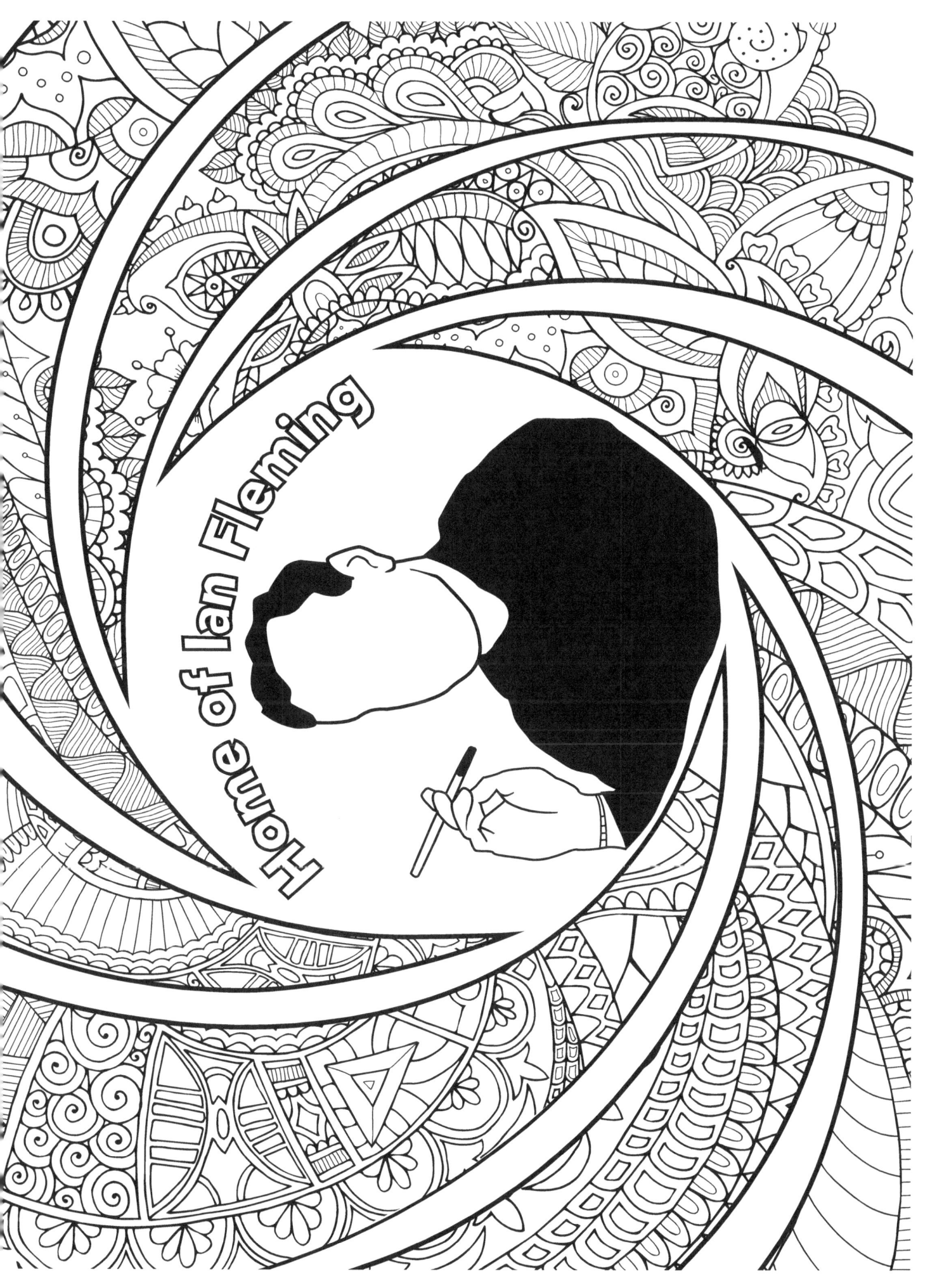

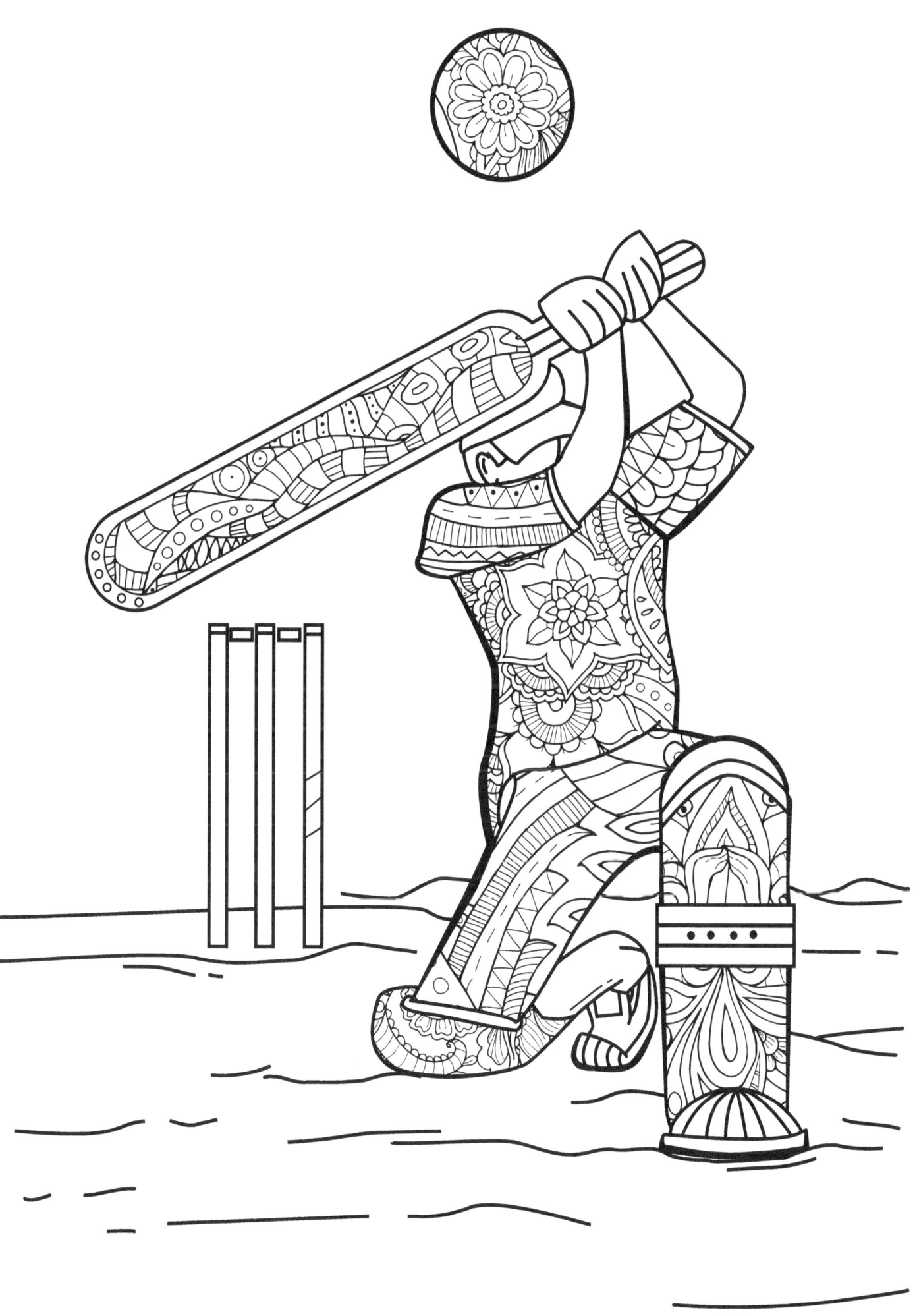

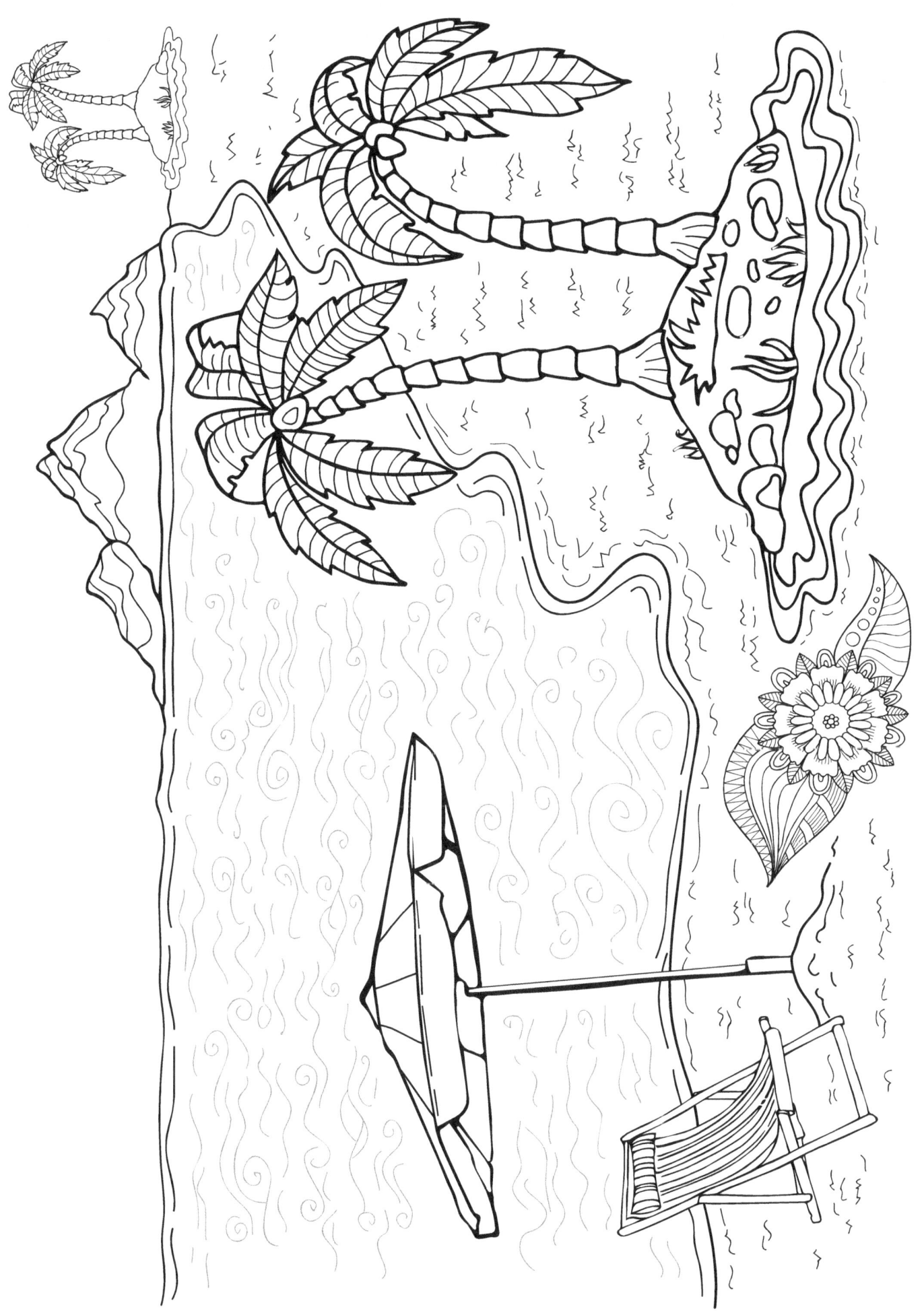

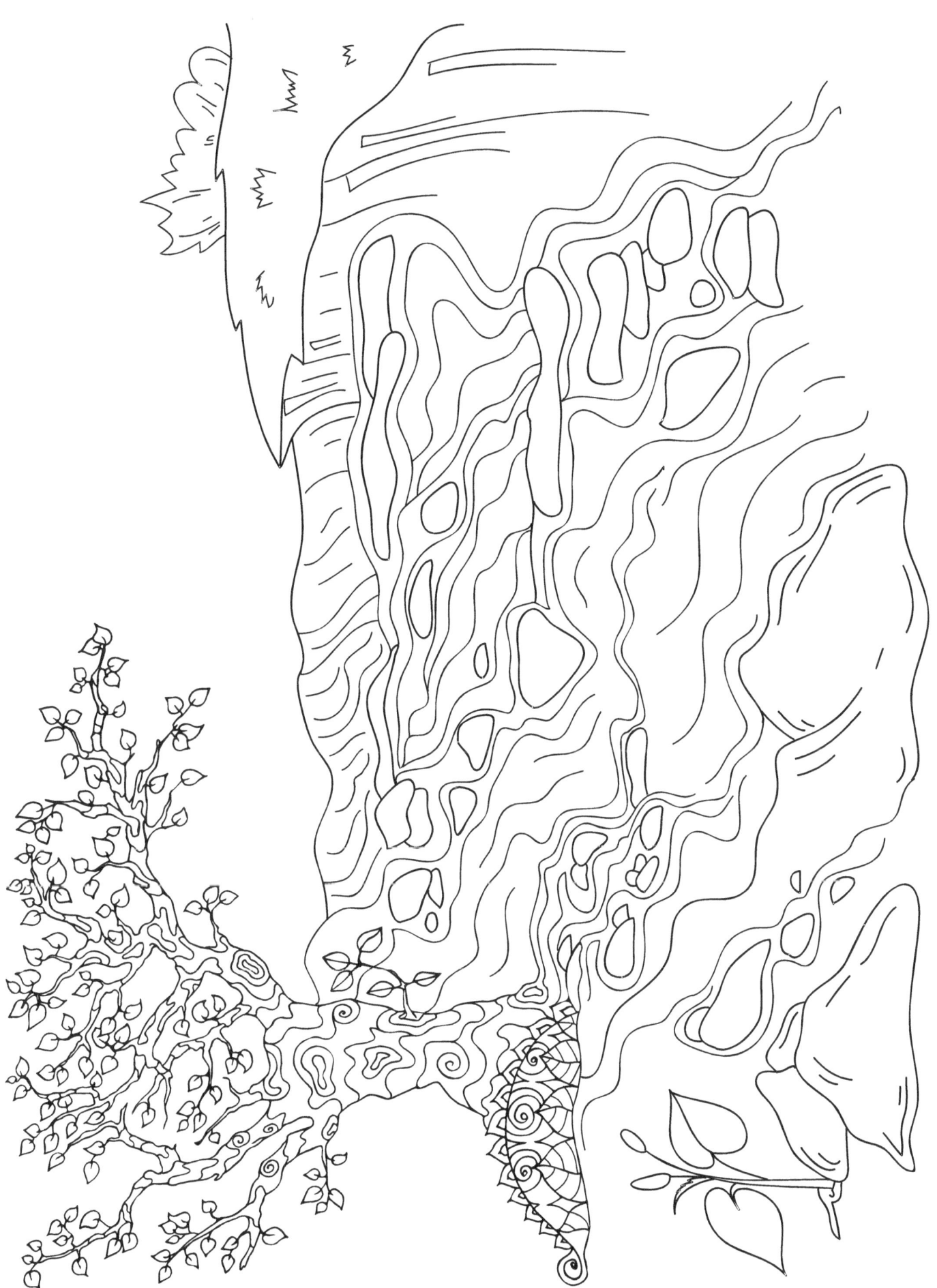

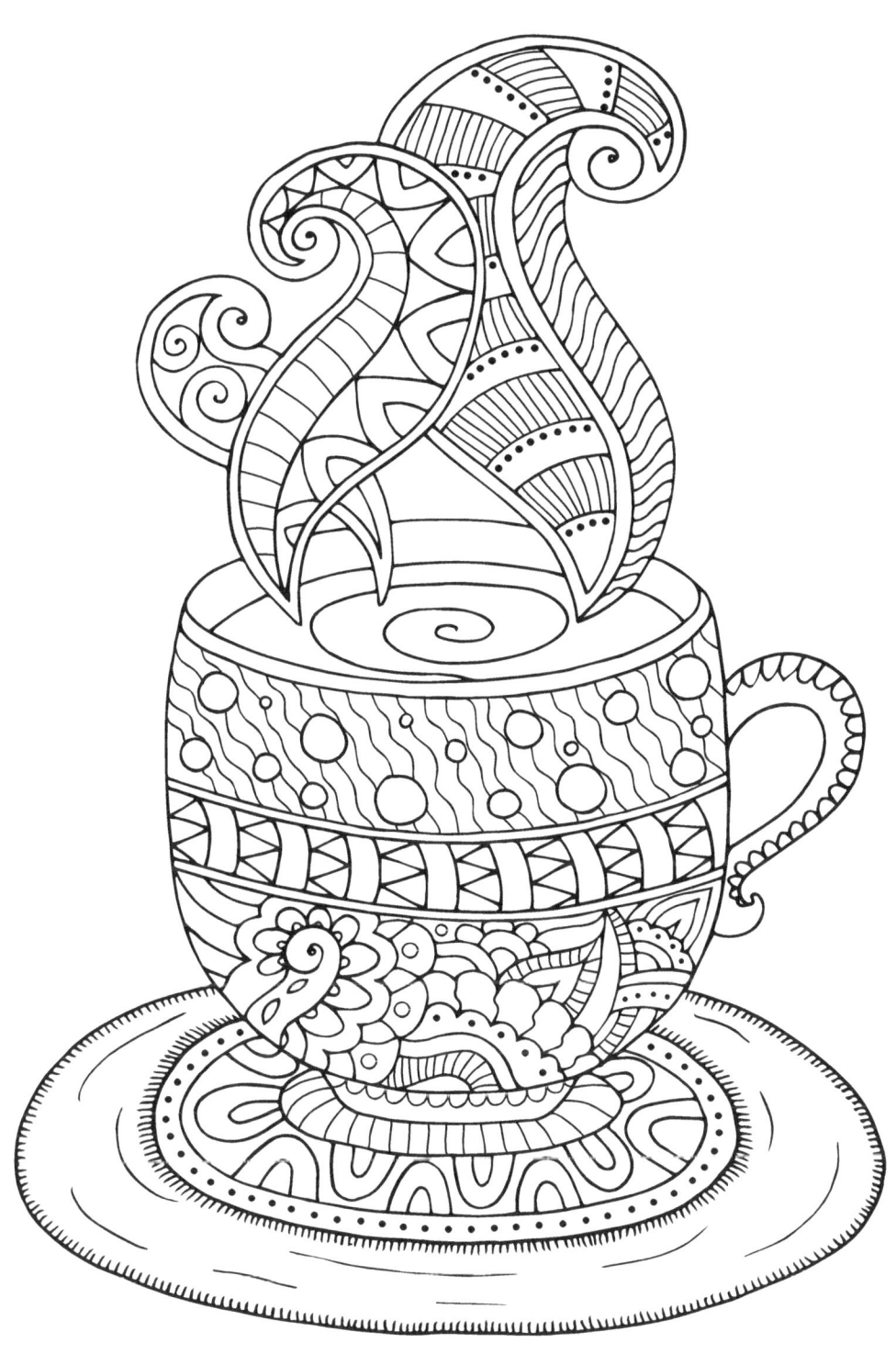

JAMAICA COFFEE

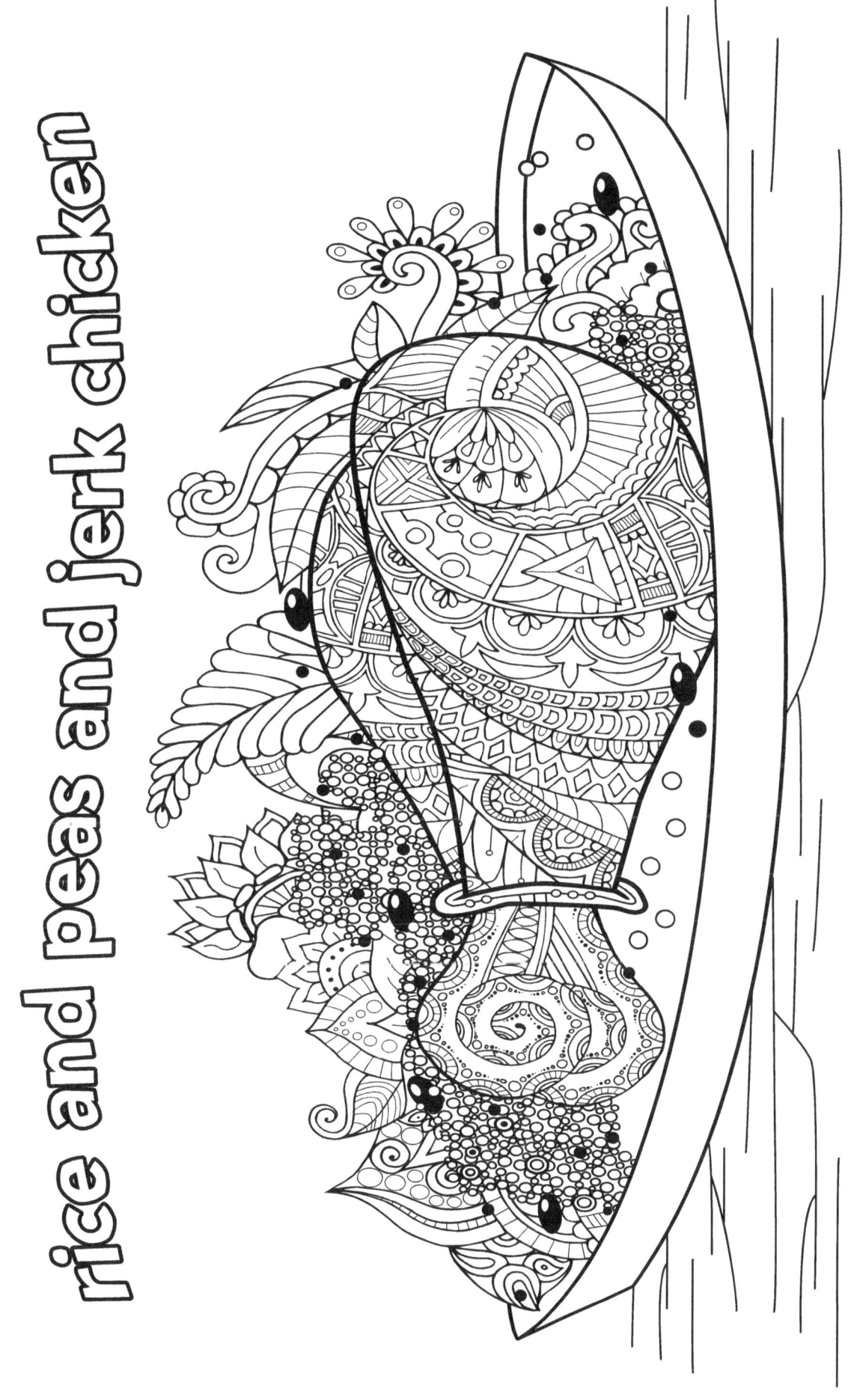

rice and peas and jerk chicken

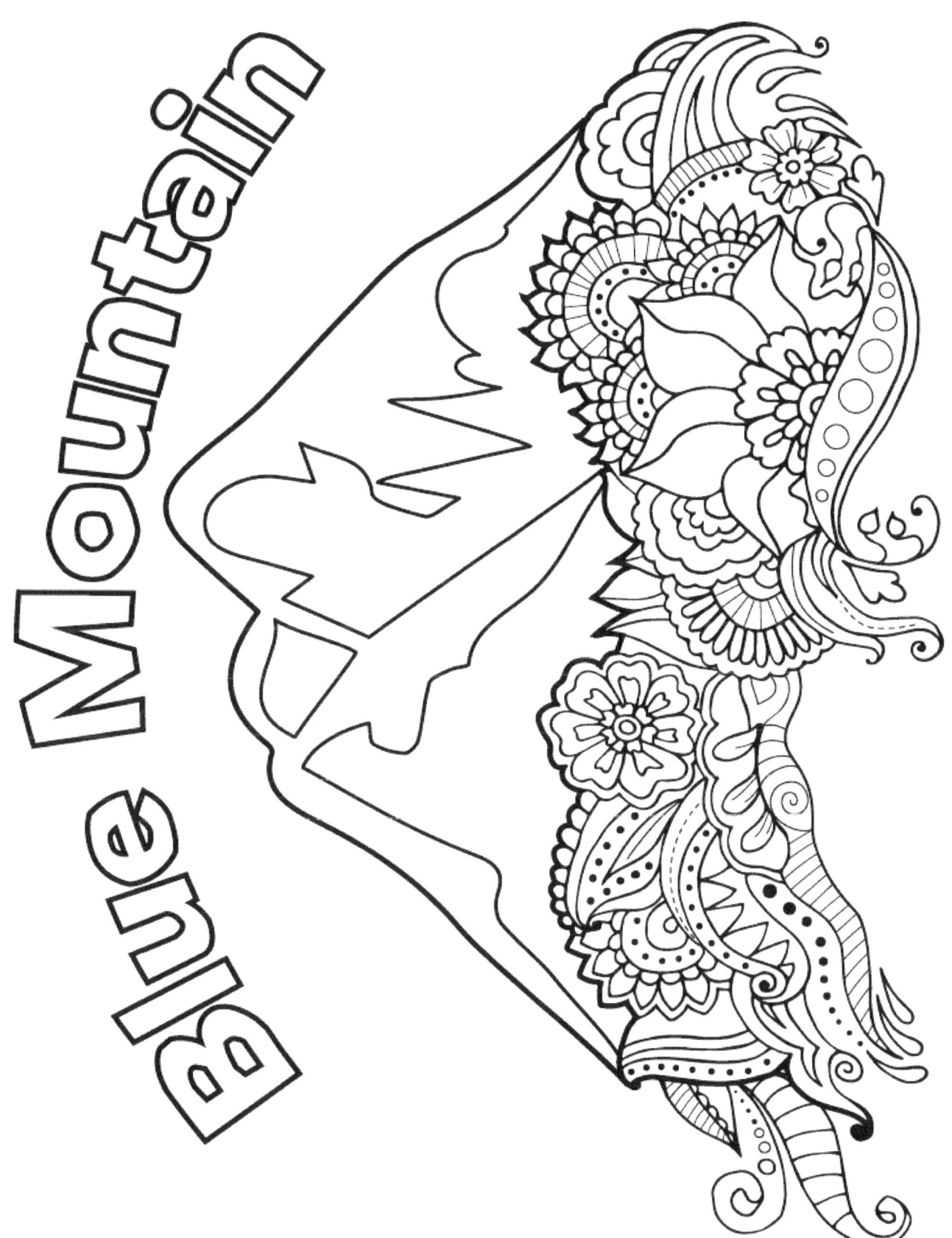

Blue Mountain

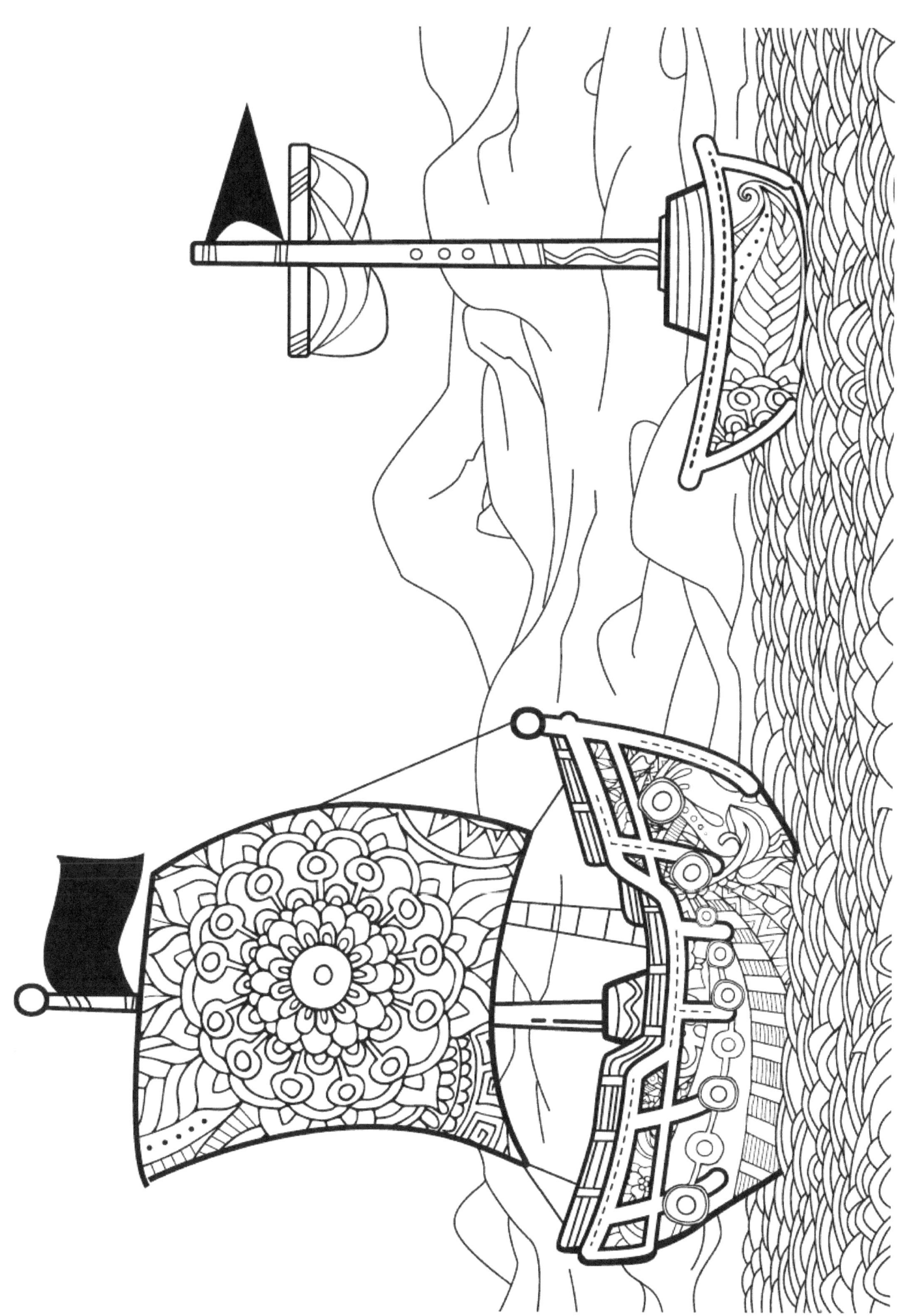

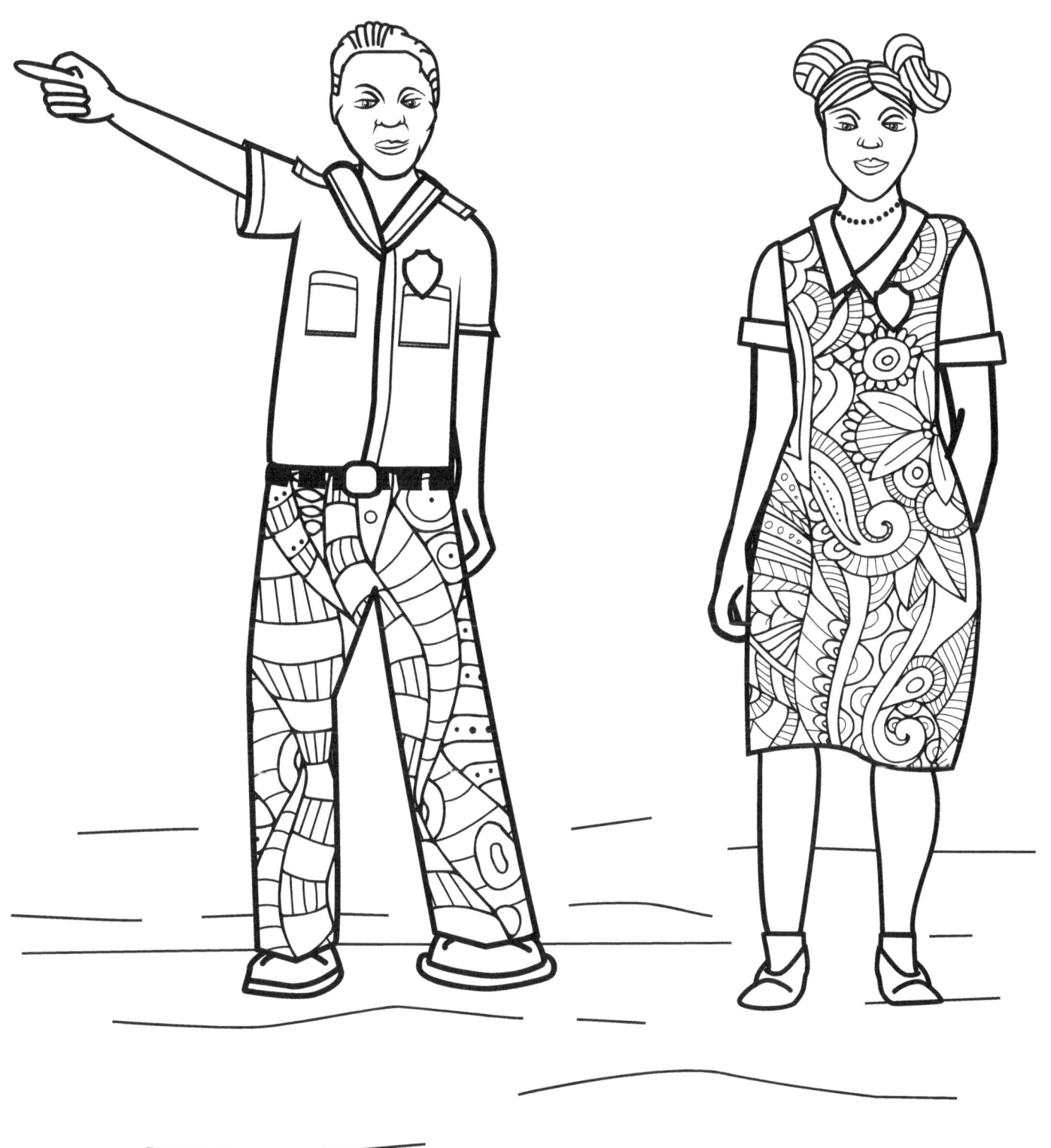

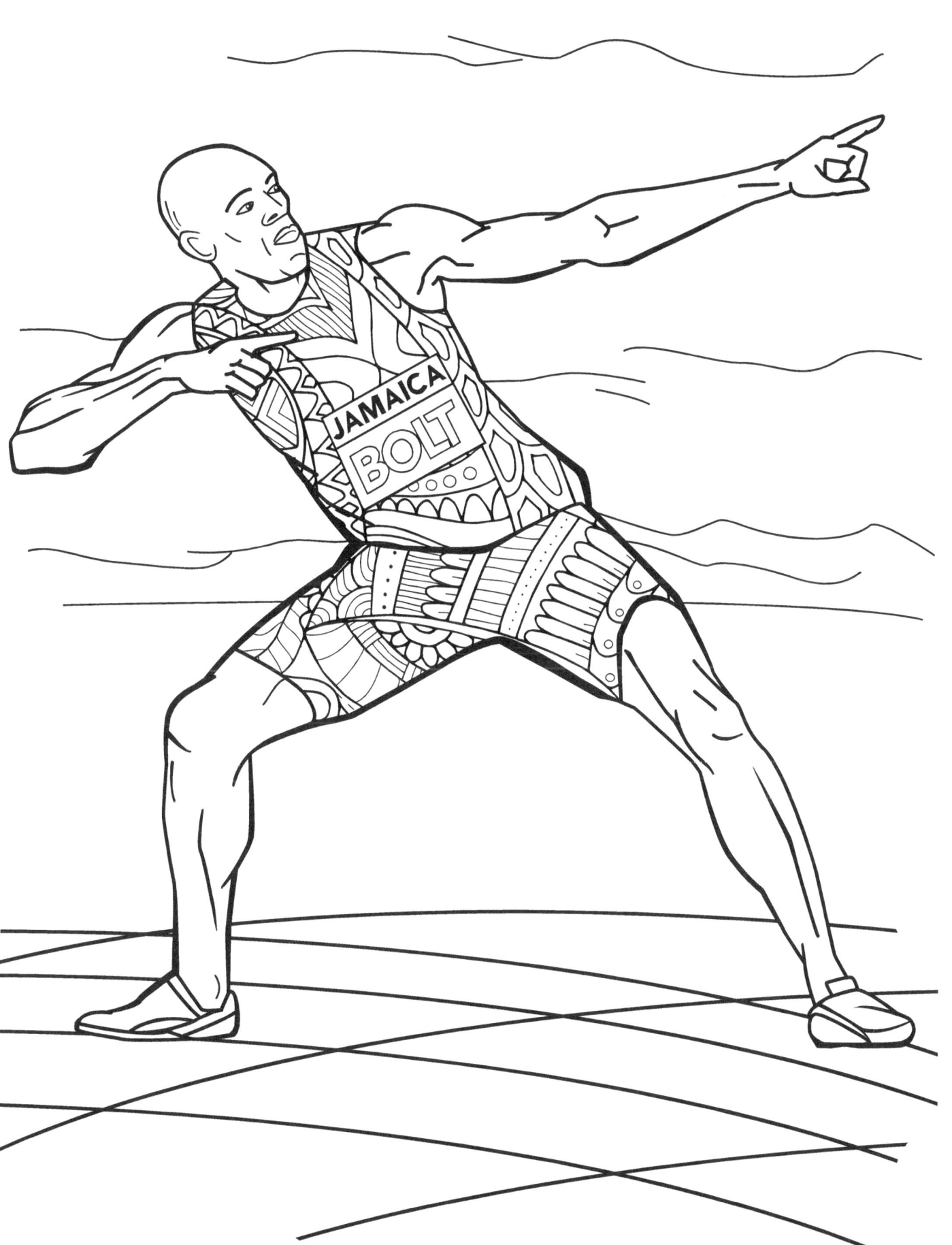

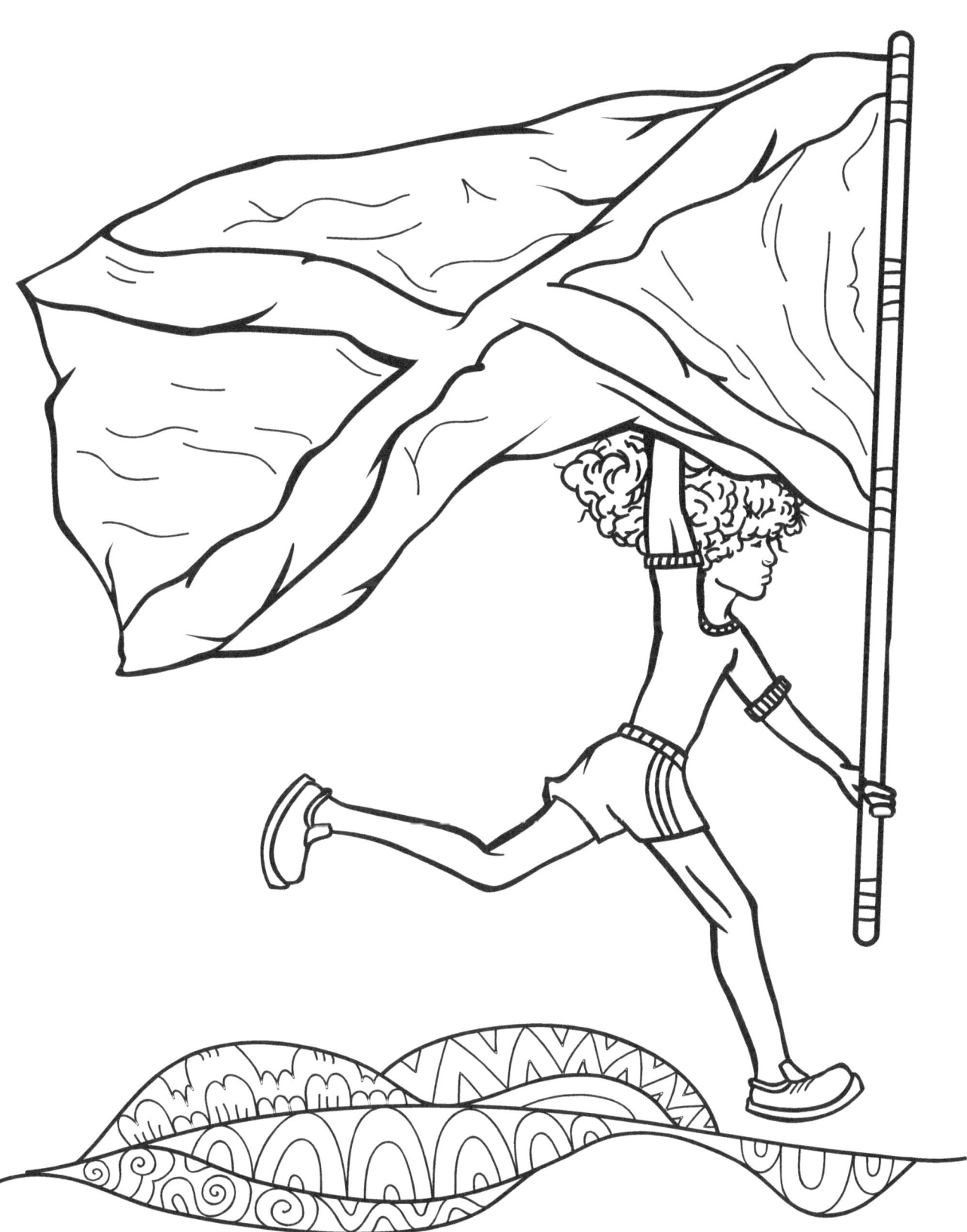

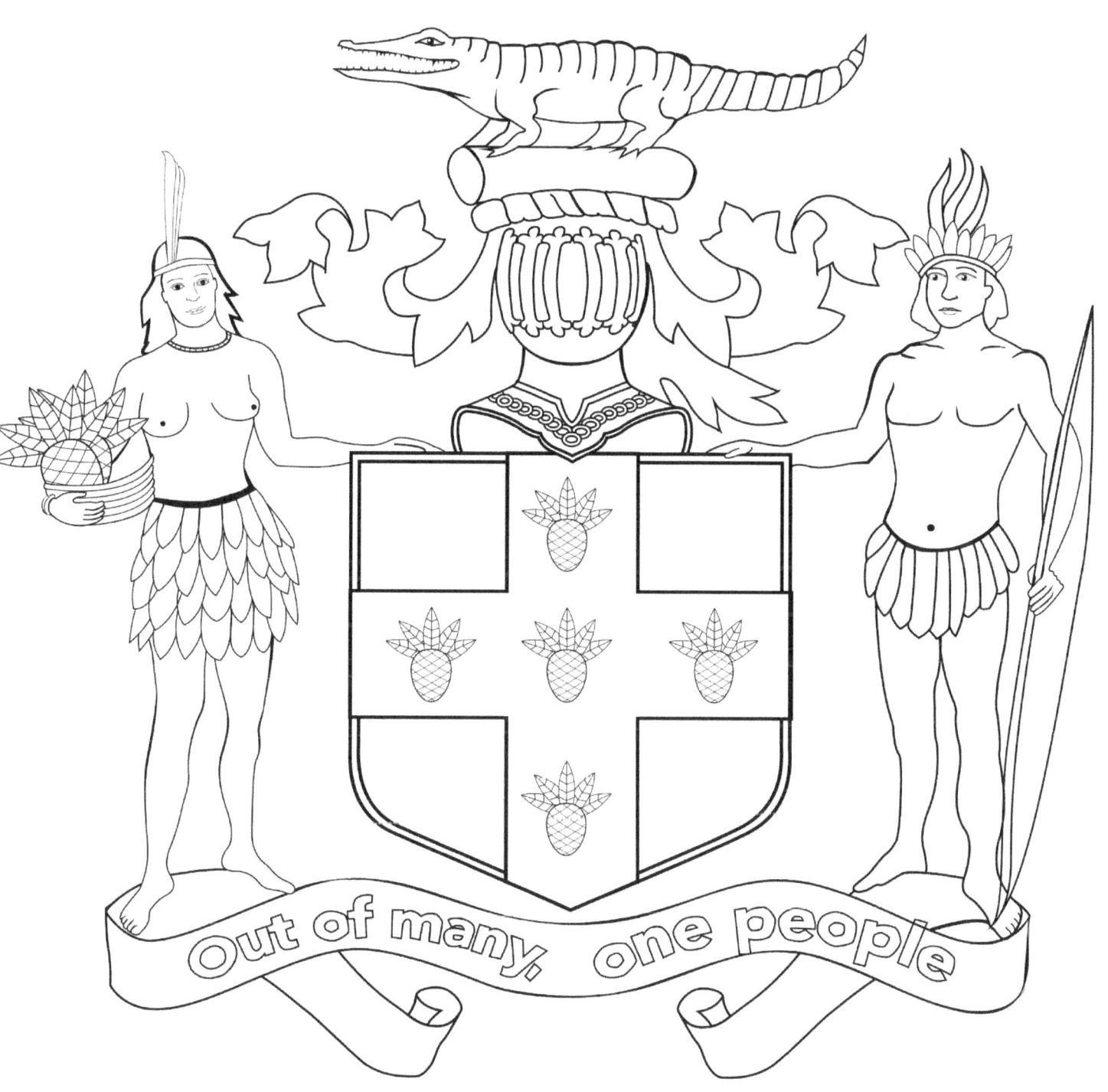

Out of many, one people

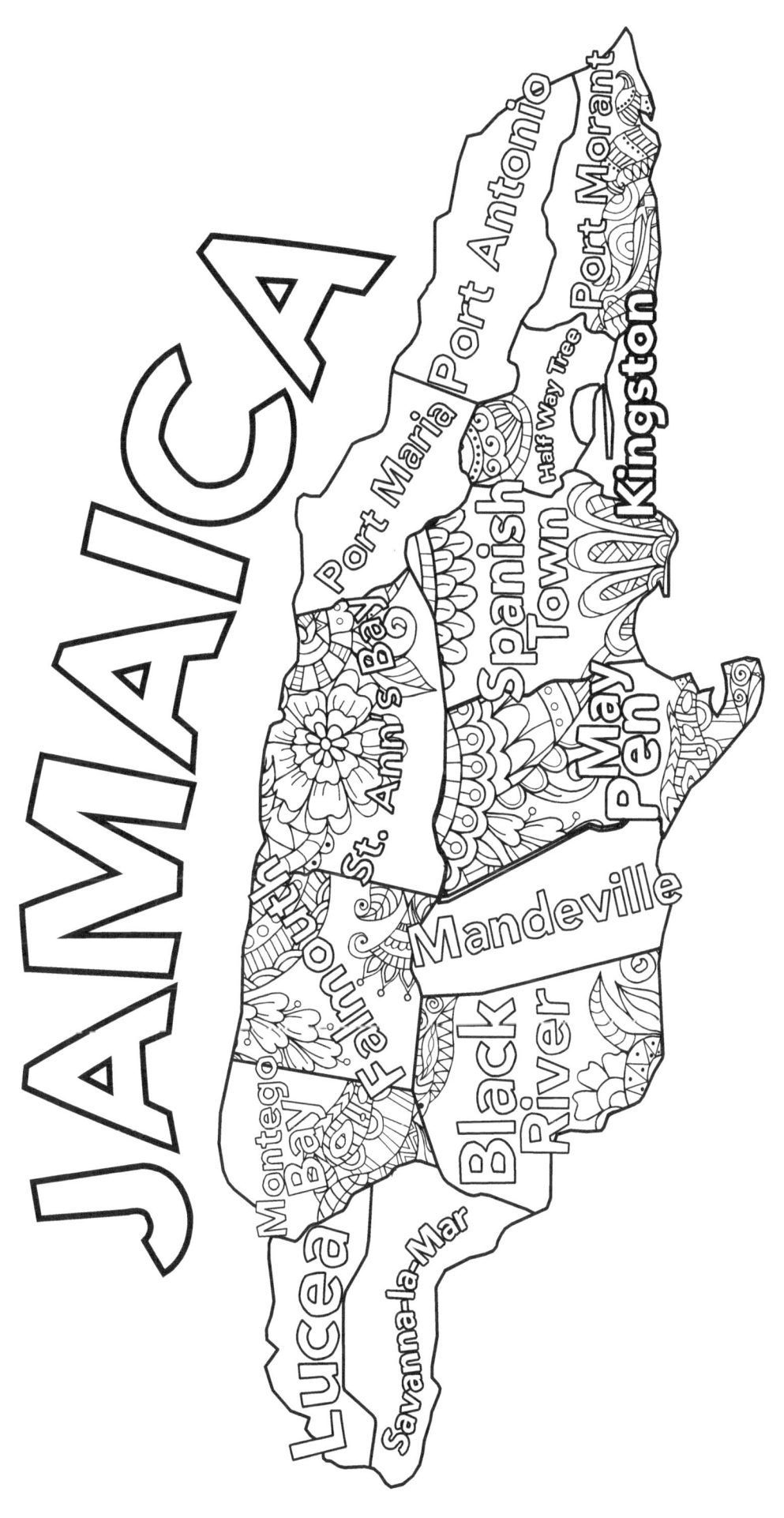

Jamaican Facts

1. "Out of Many, One people," became Jamaica's official motto following the independence of the country from Britain in 1962.

2. Contrary to what you may think, Rastafarians make up less than 1% of the total Jamaican population. Christianity is by far the most popular religion on the island.

3. There are over 200 different species of exotic orchid in Jamaica. 66 of these are indigenous to the island.

4. Kingston's harbour is the seventh largest natural harbour in the world

5. Jamaica was, in 1997, the first English speaking country of the Caribbean to qualify for the football world cup.

6. In 1988, Jamaica was the first topical country to enter a Bobsleigh team into the Winter Olympic. The story of their journey was later turned into the popular movie, "Cool Runnings".

7. The widest spoken language in Jamaica is called Patois. It is an English based language with strong West African influences. Despite it being so commonly spoken, it is not a written language- they use English instead.

8. One of Jamaica's most luxurious exports is Blue Mountain Coffee. It's highly sought-after, and is one of the rarest coffees in the world.

9. The national dish of Jamaica is Ackee, which is a type of fruit similar to a lychee.

10. Ian Fleming wrote all 14 of his James Bond novels when he was living in Jamaica. His home was called Goldeneye.

11. More than half of Jamaica's economy comes from tourism, with the rest being a mix of agriculture, mining, and manufacturing.

12. Jamaica is one of two Caribbean islands that are home to the 2nd largest butterfly in the world, the Giant Swallowtail.

13. The original people who lived on the island were known as the Taíno.

14. Reggae music originated in Jamaica. Their most famous musician, Bob Marley, toured the world along with his backing group called The Wailers. His track, "Legend", was the best-selling reggae album ever.

15. The fastest man in the world lives in Jamaica. During his career, Usain Bolt won 8 gold medals for short distance sprinting events.

16. Jamaica was the first commercial producer of bananas in the Western world.

17. The national bird of Jamaica is the Swallow-tailed hummingbird. Also known as the Doctor Bird, it only lives in Jamaica and is one of the most stunning of the 320 hummingbird species.

18. In 2012, the population of Jamaica was estimated to be around 2.9 million people. A similar number of tourists visit the island every year.

19. Jamaica is within the hurricane belt of the Atlantic Ocean. The last one to make landfall on the island was Hurricane Sandy in 2012.

20. There are very few snakes on Jamaica. This wasn't always the case, but in 1872 a population of mongooses was released to rid an infestation of rats in the sugar cane fields. They also eat virtually all of the snakes too.

Jamaica Word Search

Can you find all of the hidden words?

```
P P E D T Y S L F N X B F K R
N P C P R A S T A F A R I A N
Y S O X C I E E K C A S C A I
Y U A V M D B A S M B I F A C
D E S K H B Z G V O M L O B C
O T L Q I C L G N F O Z P Z C
L G L R P N J E Y I S G E K X
L S A O A H G R Z O M J N R X
A C H I K M O S M Y C M N O A
R V E E T D I L T C X K U G M
P T C F J N Z P G O T F O H S
V Z N L T K A Z F I N D U K Z
Y S A L T F I S H N H L S H V
Y W D Q D F P V N K A B C W B
N R N O Y V S S F R R V A C N
```

Ackee
Caribbean
Dancehall

Dollar
Hummingbird
Kingston

Marley
Mongoose
Rastafarian

Reggae
Saltfish
Santiago

Jamaica Quiz

Questions

1. When did Christopher Columbus arrive in Jamaica?
2. What was the island's main export under British colonial rule?
3. Which mountains dominate the inlands of Jamaica?
4. Jamaica lies in the hurricane belt of which Ocean?
5. How many of Jamaica's eight species of native snakes are venomous?
6. What is the most popular sport in Jamaica?
7. Jamaica was the inspiration for a number of James Bond stories, but which James Bond movie is the only one to have been set on the island?
8. The National bird of Jamaica is known as the doctor bird. What type of bird is it?
9. How many Universities are there on the island?
10. Jamaica has consistently produced world-class athletes in track   and field. What is the name of the current world record holder in the 100m for men at 9.58s, and 200m for men at 19.19s?
11. What colours appear on the Jamaican national flag?
12. Christopher Columbus claimed the island in the name of which country?
13. Other than Kingston, what is the name of the only other official city in Jamaica (known for its tourist destinations)?
14. In what year did Jamaica gain Independence?
15. The Jamaican Slider is a species of what marine animal that is native the island?
16. What is the main religion that is practised in Jamaica?
17. Which pirate became the first Lt. Governor of Jamaica?
18. Which side of the road do Jamaicans drive on?
19. Which famous person appears on the back of a Jamaican 10 cent coin?
20. Which genre of music evolved out of Ska and Rocksteady and originated in Jamaica in the 1960's?

Jamaica Crossword

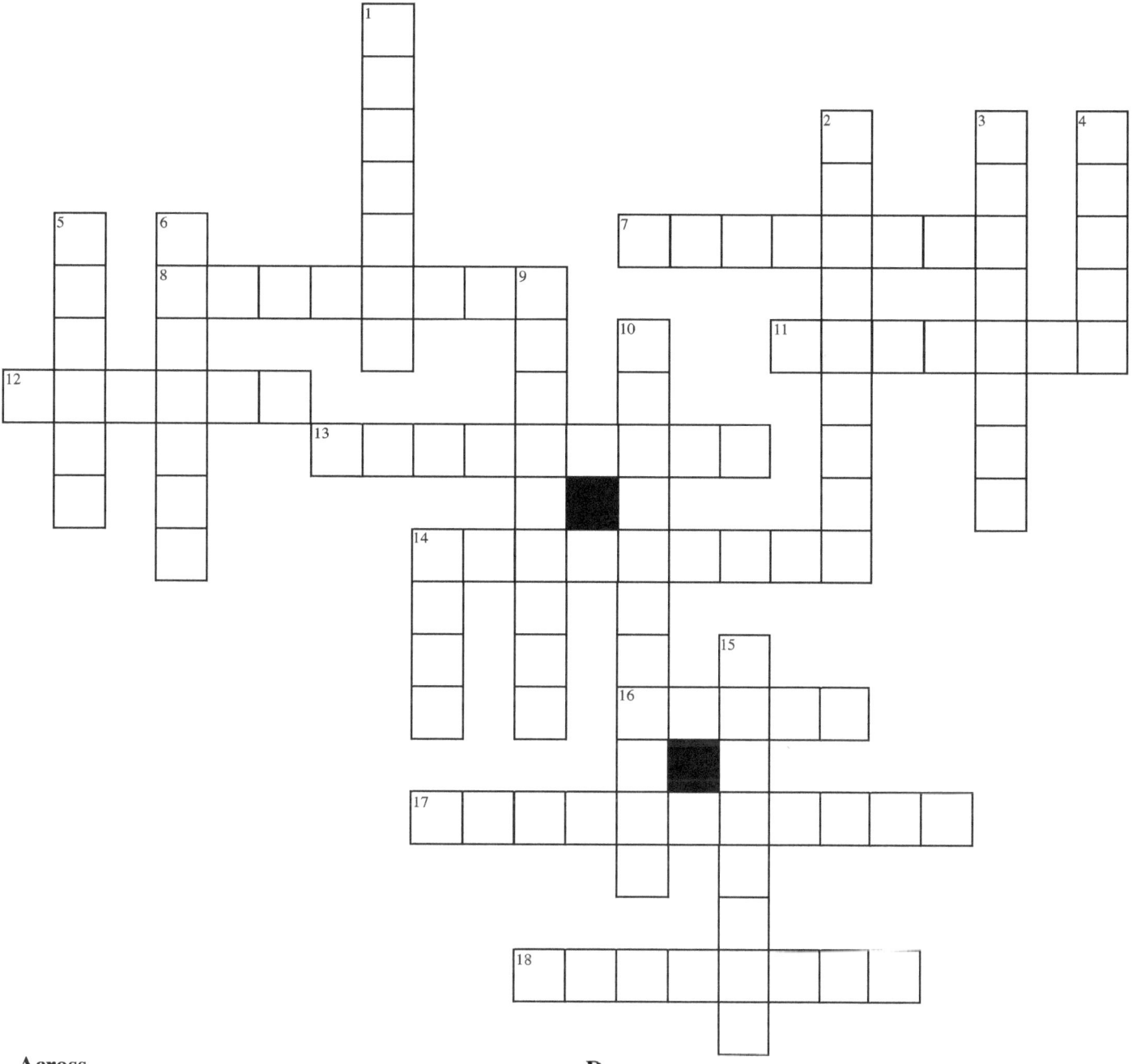

Across

7. The name Christopher Columbus first gave the island (8)
8. The Caribbean sea is in the suboceanic basin of which ocean? (8)
11. The ore of aluminium found in central Jamaica (7)
12. Currency of Jamaica (6)
13. What severe weather condition does Jamaica regularly face? (9)
14. The sport in which Jamaica first entered the Winter Olympics (9)
16. The name of the original people of Jamaica (5)
17. National bird of Jamaica (11)
18. Mammal that feeds on rats and snakes, prevalent on the island since its introduction in 1872 (8)

Down

1. Ian _____, creator of James Bond who lived on the island (7)
2. The name of the English monarch who is Head of State (9)
3. Jamaica's longest river (3, 5)
4. National fruit of Jamaica (5)
5. Dominant spoken language in Jamaica (6)
6. Backing singers for Bob Marley, The _____ (7)
9. Jamaica is the 3rd largest island in which sea? (9)
10. The name of the 2nd largest butterfly in the world (11)
14. Primary Colour and name of the most famous Jamaican mountain (4)
15. The capital city of Jamaica (8)

Spot The Difference

6 Differences to Spot. Can You Spot Them All?

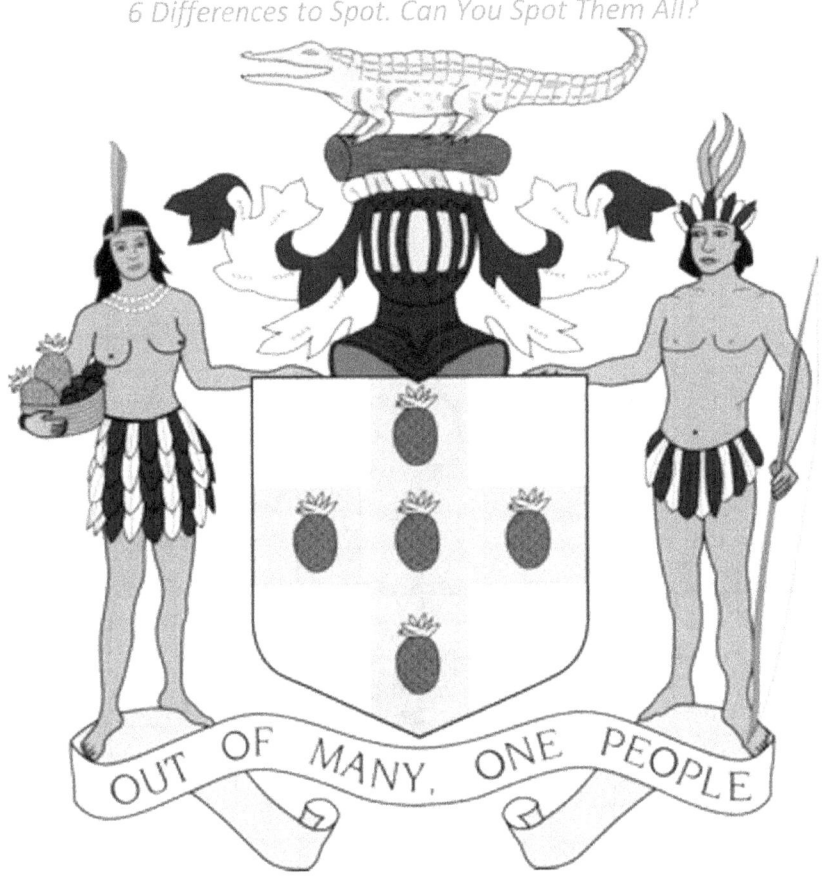

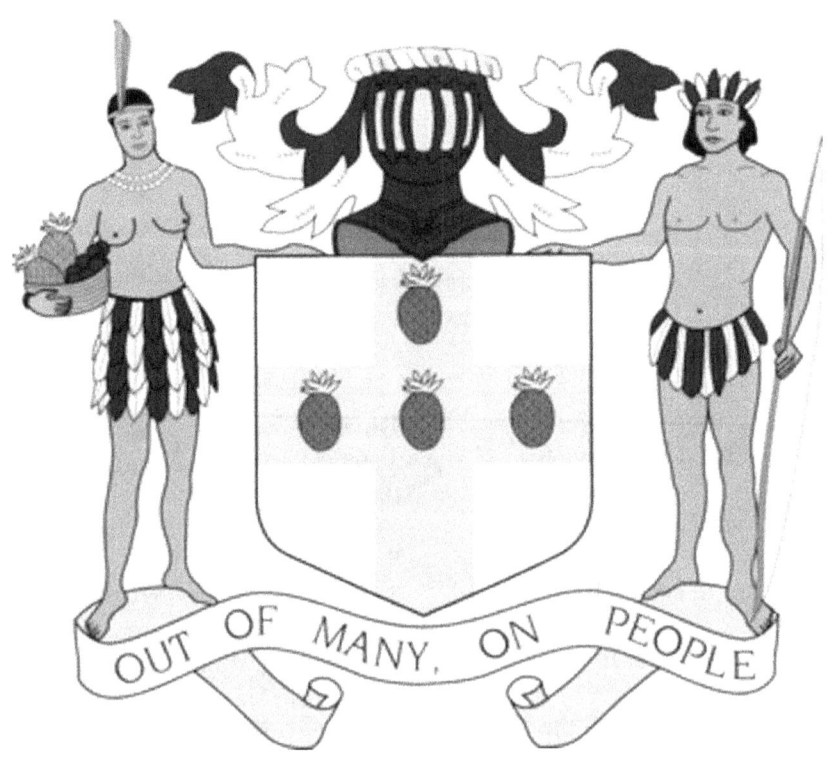

Jamaica Word Search

Can you find all of the hidden words?

```
P P E D T Y S L F N X B F K R
N P C P R A S T A F A R I A N
Y S O X C I E E K C A S C A I
Y U A V M D B A S M B I F A C
D E S K H B Z G V O M L O B C
O T L Q I C L G N F O Z P Z C
L G L R P N J E Y I S G E K X
L S A O A H G R Z O M J N R X
A C H I K M O S M Y C M N O A
R V E E T D I L T C X K U G M
P T C F J N Z P G O T F O H S
V Z N L T K A Z F I N D U K Z
Y S A L T F I S H N H L S H V
Y W D Q D F P V N K A B C W B
N R N O Y V S S F R R V A C N
```

Ackee

Caribbean

Dancehall

Dollar

Hummingbird

Kingston

Marley

Mongoose

Rastafarian

Reggae

Saltfish

Santiago

Answers

1. 1494
2. Sugar
3. The Blue Mountains
4. Atlantic Ocean
5. None
6. Cricket
7. Doctor No
8. Hummingbird
9. 5
10. Usain Bolt
11. Black, Gold and Green
12. Spain
13. Montego Bay
14. 1962
15. Freshwater Turtle
16. Christianity
17. Sir Henry Morgan
18. The left
19. Jamaican National Hero and Jamaican Baptist deacon, Paul Bogle
20. Reggae

Spot The Difference

1. Female Hair
2. Words E Missing
3. Pineapple
4. Crocodile
5. Male Headdress
6. Jewel on Royal Helmet

Thank you for purchasing this book.

If you would like to know more about Aryla Publishing Books please visit:-

www.ArylaPublishing.com

Or follow us on
Facebook
Twitter
Instagram
for *free promotions*

@arylapublishing

We would love to know what you think of this book so please leave us a review.

Have a wonderful day ☺

Other Coloring Books from Aryla Publishing

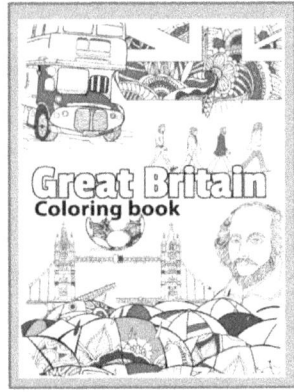
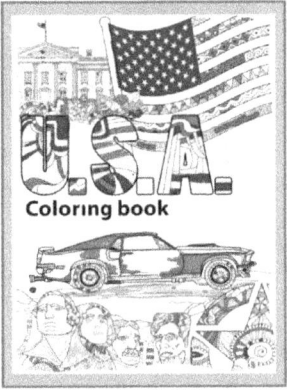
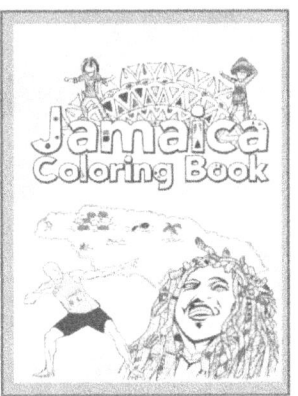
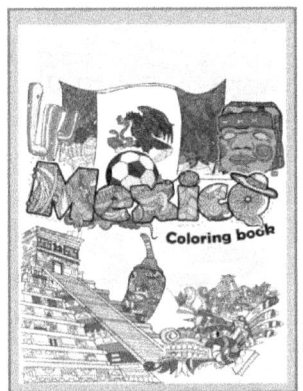

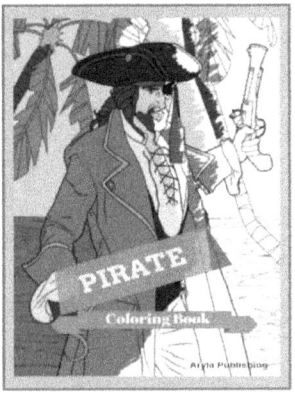
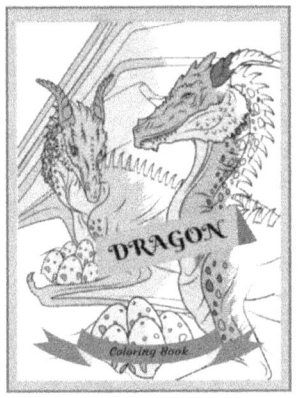
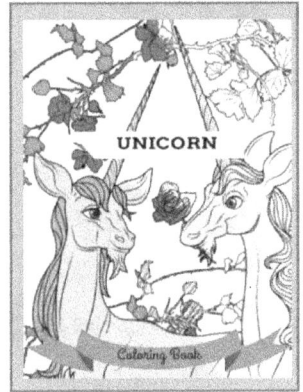
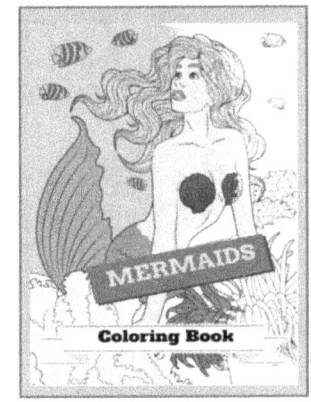

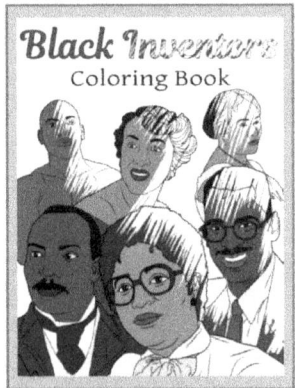
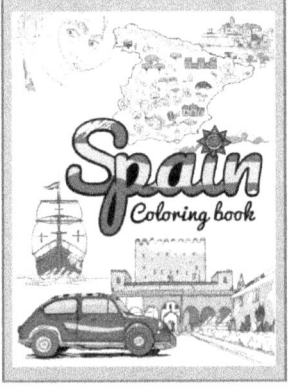
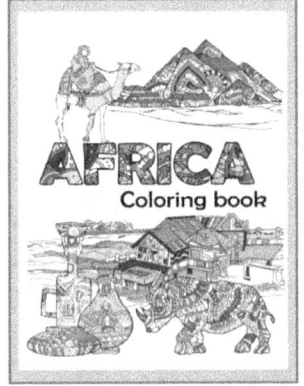
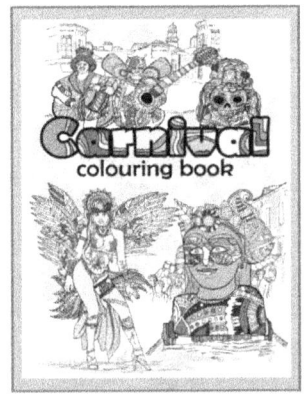

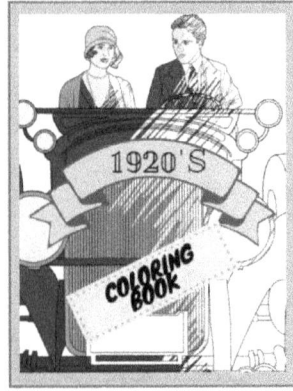
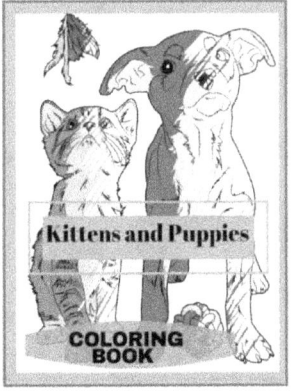
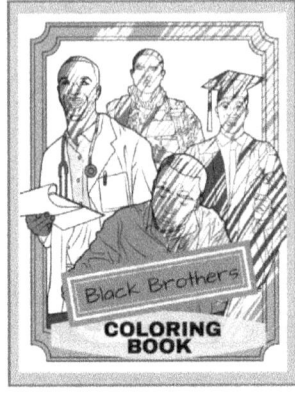
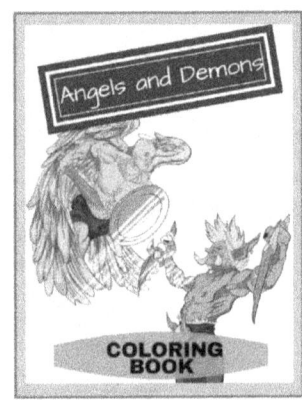

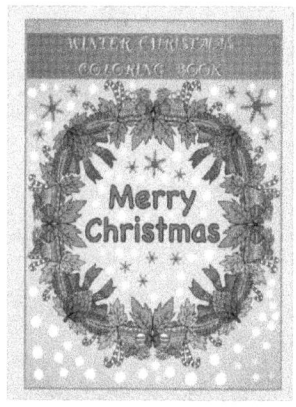
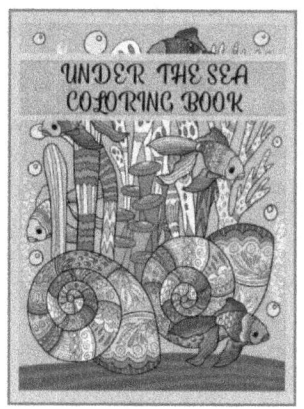
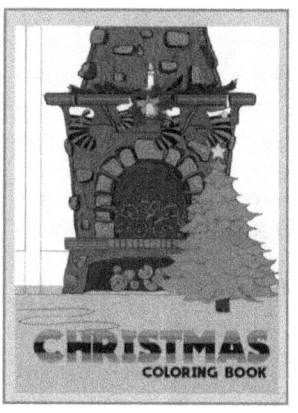
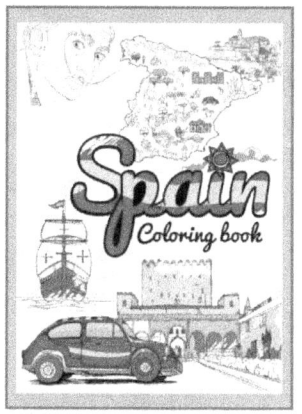
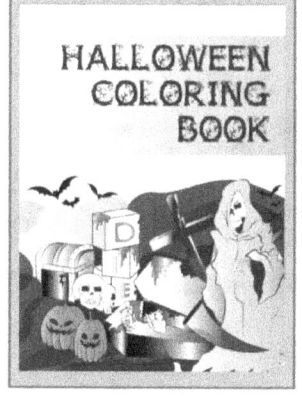
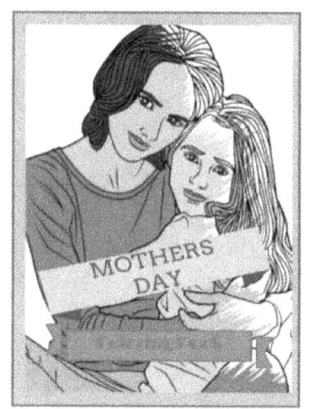
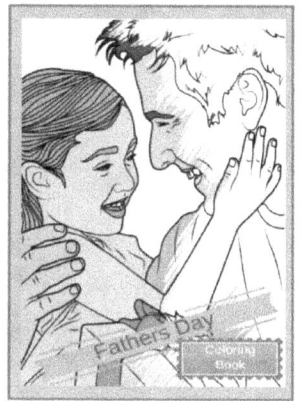
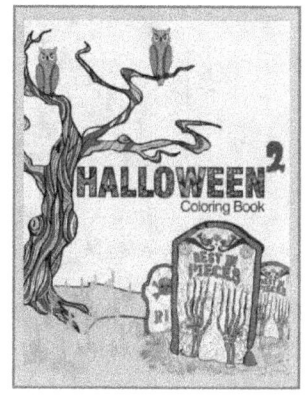
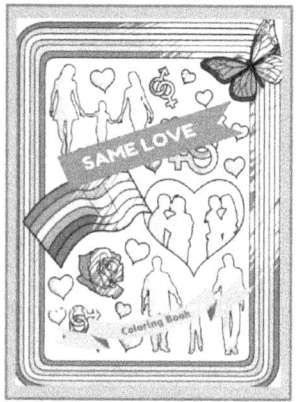
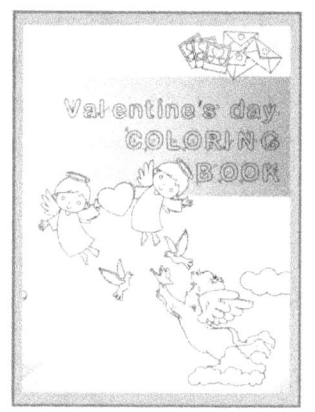
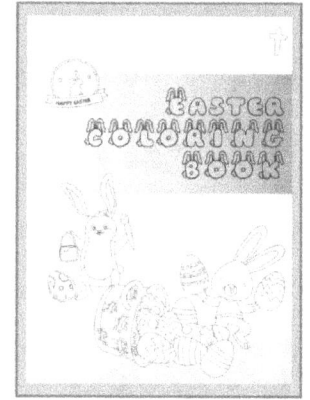
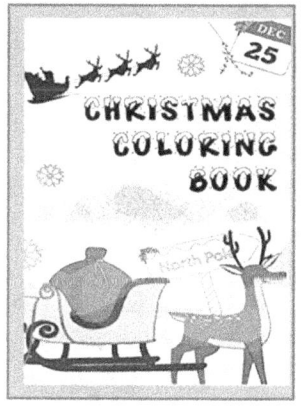

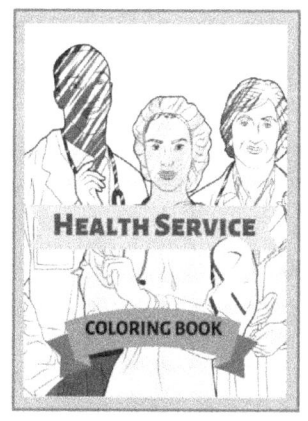
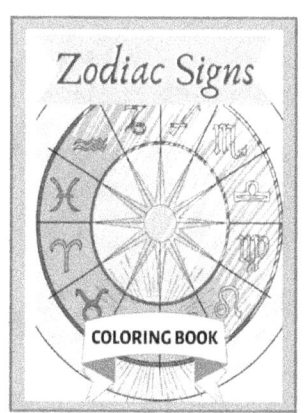
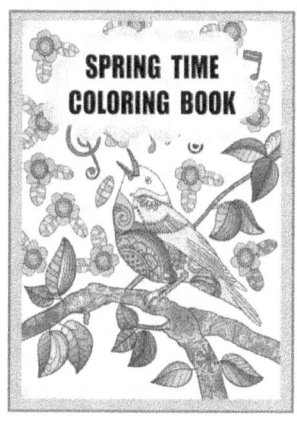

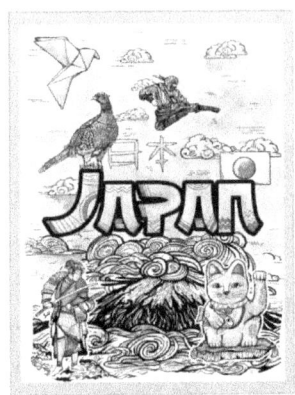

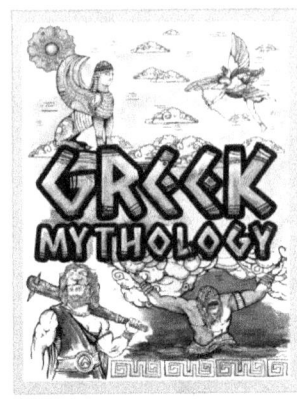

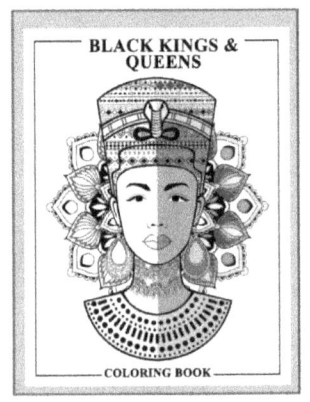

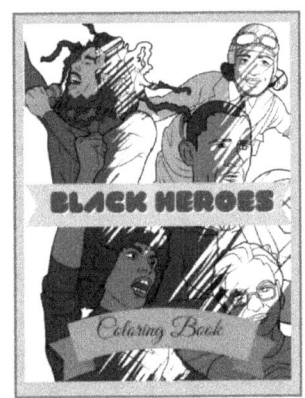

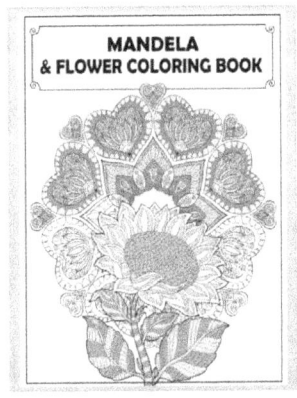

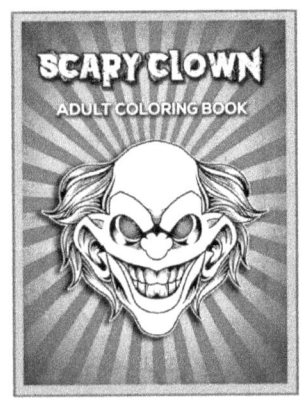

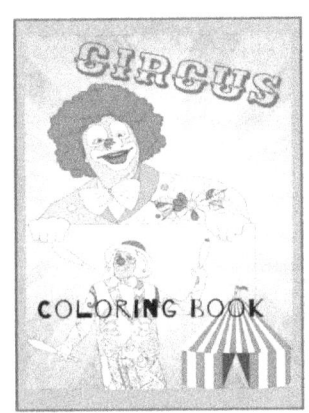

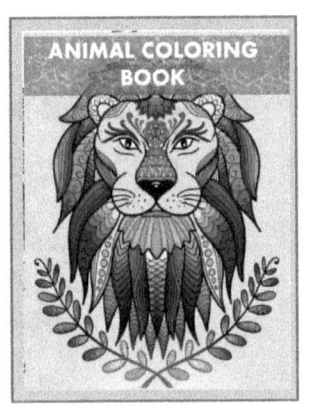

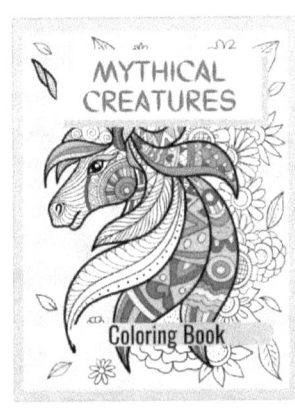

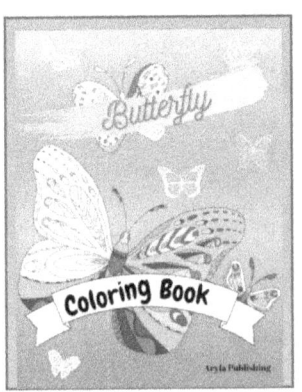

Color In Fun
Kids Books

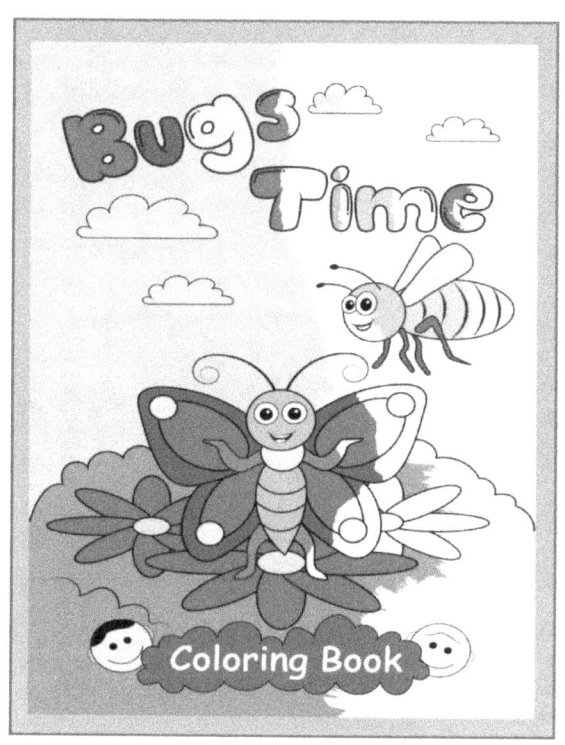

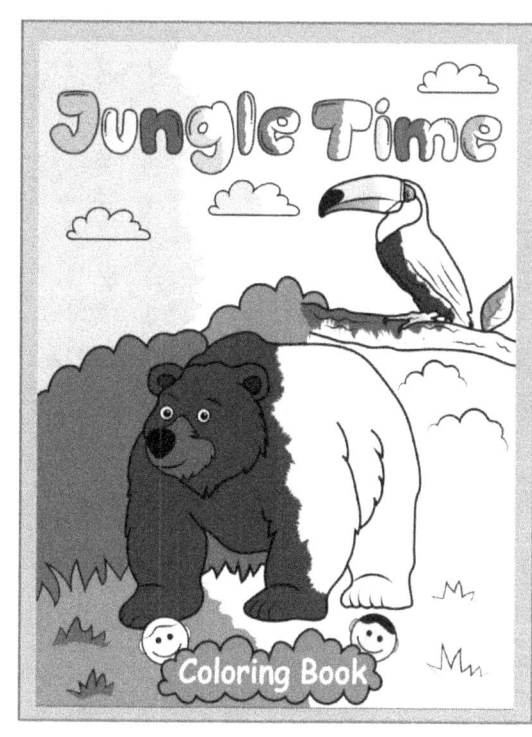

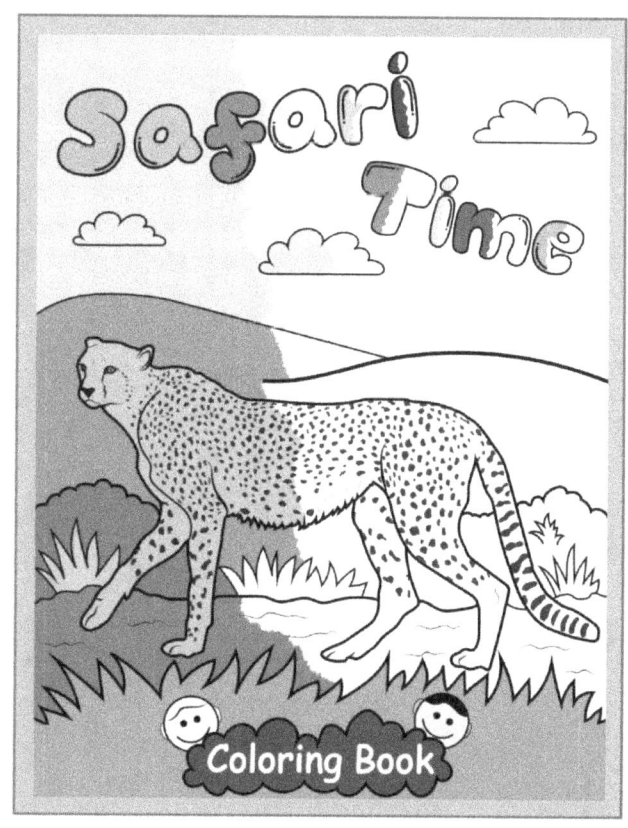

Visit **www.ArylaPublishing.com**

to find out about all new releases.

Follow us @arylapublishing on Twitter Instagram & Facebook

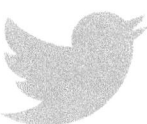  

Search for Aryla Publishing on

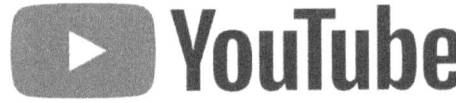 **YouTube**

Check out our <u>Book Trailers</u>

<u>Subscribe</u> to keep up to date with new releases!

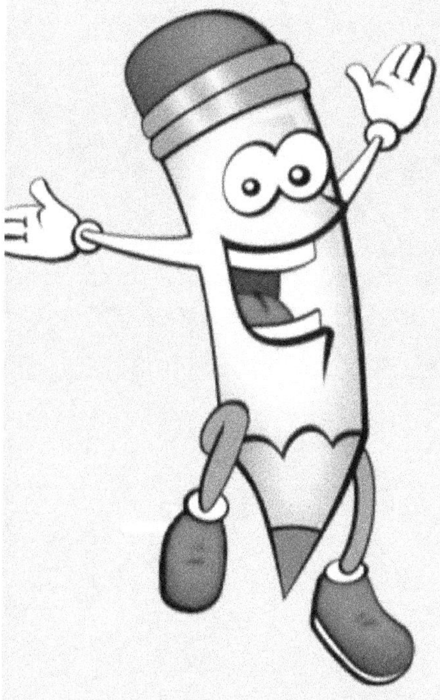

WE WOULD LOVE YOUR FEEDBACK

PLEASE LEAVE REVIEW AT:-

https://bit.ly/Jamaicareview

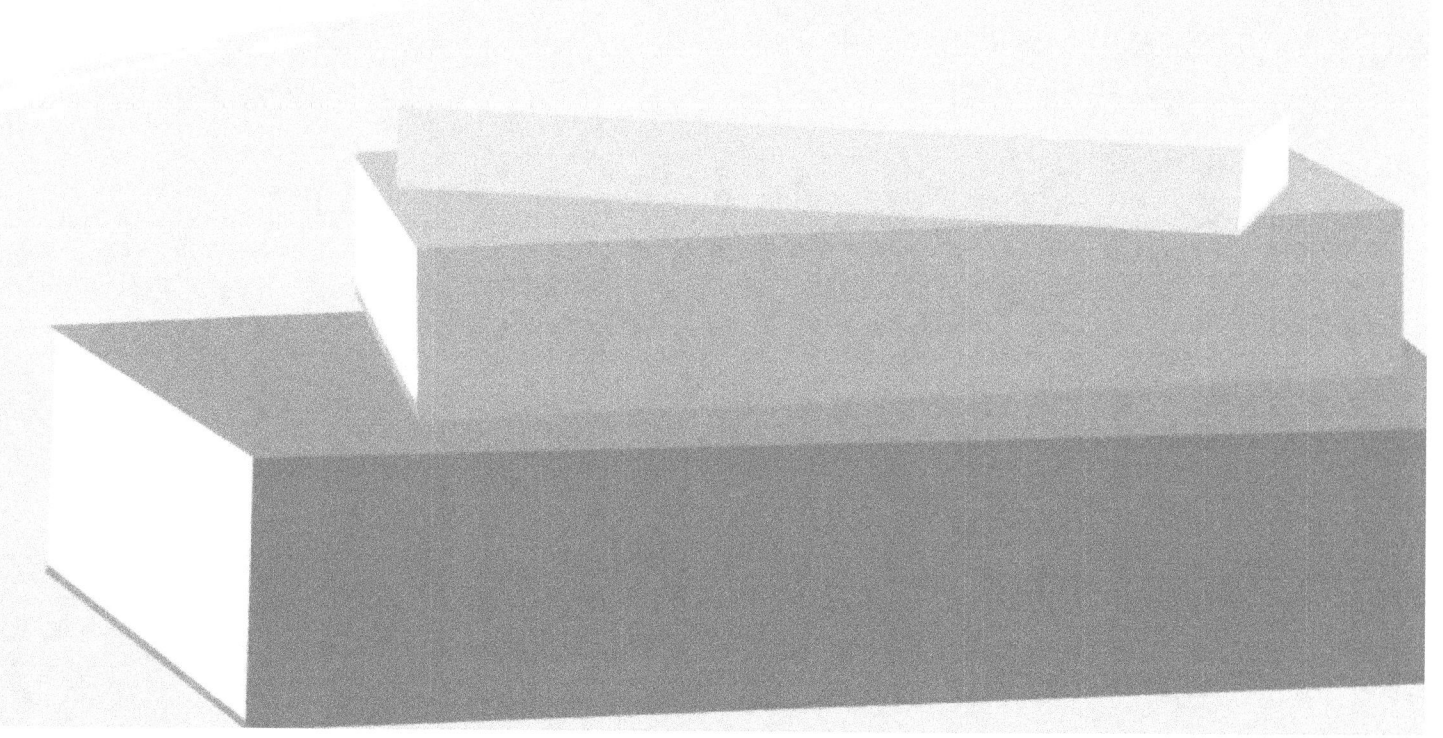

www.ingramcontent.com/pod-product-compliance
Lightning Source LLC
Chambersburg PA
CBHW081740220526
45468CB00008B/2185